JOURNEY

TO FREEDOM

Your Start to a Lifetime of
Hope, Health, and Happiness

SCOTT REALL
YMCA OF MIDDLE TENNESSEE

THOMAS NELSON
Since 1798

NASHVILLE   DALLAS   MEXICO CITY   RIO DE JANEIRO   BEIJING

Published in Nashville, Tennessee, by Thomas Nelson. Thomas Nelson is a registered trademark of Thomas Nelson, Inc.

Thomas Nelson, Inc., titles may be purchased in bulk for educational, business, fund-raising, or sales promotional use. For information, please e-mail SpecialMarkets@ThomasNelson.com.

Unless otherwise indicated, all Scripture references are from the New Century Version®. © 2005 by Thomas Nelson, Inc. Used by permission. All rights reserved.

Scripture references marked KJV are taken from the KING JAMES VERSION.

Scripture references marked NKJV are from THE NEW KING JAMES VERSION. © 1982 by Thomas Nelson, Inc. Used by permission. All rights reserved.

Scripture references marked NIV are from HOLY BIBLE: NEW INTERNATIONAL VERSION®. NIV®. ©1973, 1978, 1984 by International Bible Society. Used by permission of Zondervan Publishing House. All rights reserved.

To find a YMCA near you, please visit the following Web sites:

United States of America: www.ymca.com
Canada: www.ymca.ca
Trouvez votre YMCA: www.ymca.ca/fre_findy.htm
England: www.ymca.org.uk
Australia: www.ymca.org.au

If you would like to invite Scott to speak to your church, community organization, or YMCA, please visit www.journeytofreedom.org.

If you would like to be trained as a facilitator to start Journey to Freedom groups in your church, community organization, or YMCA, please visit www.restoreymca.org.

If you would like to donate to Restore Ministries of the YMCA of Middle Tennessee to help support the life-changing work of this ministry, please visit www.restoreymca.org/donate-restore.

ISBN 978-1-4185-3571-1

Printed in the United States of America
19 20 21 22 23 LSC 53 52 51 50 49

CONTENTS

ACKNOWLEDGMENTS

This book was an amazing journey with God—a true testimony to how God does things for us that we cannot do for ourselves. This book would not have been possible if it were not for the efforts of many wonderful people who spent countless hours making these thoughts come to life.

Robbie Stoffel and Lori Jones from Thomas Nelson Publishers, you captured my voice!

Laura Amstutz, Adora Bruce, Heather Lawrence, Melissa Osterloo, Tilly Cryar, and Lindsey Campbell, you were God's gift to me to get this book written. I could never have gotten it done without your help. Thank you, thank you, thank you.

A special thanks to Rebecca Griffith and Lindsey Castleman for your great input and insights on the revisions for *Journey to Freedom*. It is now better than I could have imagined.

Charlie Newman, Debra Clements, and Julie Huneycutt, thank you for your valuable input.

Rebecca Whitlock, thank you for believing in me. Your vision for this project brought it to life.

YMCA of Middle Tennessee, your support, encouragement, and belief in this project made it possible.

Mike O'Neil, God used your book to save my life.

My mom and dad, for always believing in me.

Heather, for your love.

Tony, Nikki, and Scottie, my children, I am so blessed by each of you.

Sheryl Cook, Al Stewart, and Farrah Moore, you truly are angels.

Mostly I would like to thank Jesus for Your grace—it set me free and gave me wings.

Everyone desires a lifetime of hope, health, and happiness. And in some ways, we all believe that we haven't attained it. We long for areas of our life to change. We long for freedom—freedom from our addictions, freedom from worry, freedom from debt, freedom from overeating, or freedom to choose a different career—even if it means that we have to go back to school. All of us seek a happy life, but many of us don't know how to begin to find it. Too many obstacles have blocked our way. We've made mistakes. Regrets have formed. Escape led nowhere, while blaming others only entrapped us more. We all eventually reach a place of exhaustion and need a new vision for life.

This book is designed to help you contemplate change. Psychiatrist and spiritual counselor Gerald May writes, "How much can I respect myself if I do not even know what I really want?"[1] Contemplation is the tool that we use to get an idea of the life we've always wanted. This is a difficult task to accomplish alone. We need a guide. We need a way to pinpoint the broken areas, the areas in need of change. This is the purpose of *Journey to Freedom*. It will guide you to a new life and provide some answers as to why life has not turned out the way you'd planned. We'll make suggestions, but self-examination is the way that you'll get the most out of this study.

The Bible says, "If you want to build a tower, you first sit down and decide how much it will cost, to see if you have enough money to finish the job. If you don't, you might lay the foundation, but you would not be able to finish."[2] This book is a blueprint that will assist you in counting the cost of change. The last thing we want is for you to lay a foundation of change and then run out of steam before reaching your goals, so we created this book to help you get off to a strong start on your journey to freedom.

The YMCA has been fortunate to be involved in great programs of change. YMCA staff invented basketball and volleyball. The first pro-football team was organized at the YMCA. Bodybuilding, racquetball, Father's Day, the Gideons, Toastmasters, softball, swimming and aquatics, group child care, and the Boy Scouts of America have all been either started at the YMCA or influenced by it. This is why I collaborated with the YMCA to establish Restore Ministries as a core outreach program of the YMCA of Middle Tennessee. I knew that the combined efforts for change would result in hundreds of changed lives, and it has. Restore has grown from just fifty participants in 2000 to over two thousand participants to date. Regardless of the participants' issues, they established boundaries, defeated obsessions, improved their relationships, regained hope, and grew stronger in spirit.

Parts of the study will combine Restore's process of change with the events that led to the invention of basketball at the YMCA training school in Springfield, Massachusetts, the invention of volleyball at the YMCA in Holyoke, Massachusetts, and the invention of racquetball in 1950 at the Greenwich, Connecticut, YMCA. But this is not a history book. It's about change. It's about your life. It's a blueprint to build a new beginning. This revolutionary program of change contains six days in a week, for a total of thirty-six days.

Dr. James Prochaska, author of *Changing for Good*, believes that there are six well-defined stages of change: pre-contemplation, contemplation, preparation, action, maintenance, and termination. For the next thirty-six days, we will focus on the first three stages—pre-contemplation, contemplation, and preparation. Only 20 percent of people with problems are ready to change, but more than 90 percent of behavior change programs are solely for those 20 percent of people already prepared to move forward.[3] Because of that, this book is about contemplating change. In the thirty-six days, we'll do nothing but contemplate how to change, when to change, what to change, and where change needs to occur, and at the end of the thirty-six days, you can decide to continue the journey by writing a Plan of Action for your new life—or you can decide to keep the life you have. The choice is yours.

So relax. You're contemplating a journey to freedom. Listen to your spirit, your mind, and your body. Let them lead you to a new vision for life.

UNDERSTANDING THE GOING DEEPER QUESTIONS

At the end of each day's readings, you will find a section called Going Deeper. This section will help you process, explore, and put into action what you just experienced. Going Deeper is designed for those who want to spend more time getting to know God and themselves. It is not required—but it is worth the extra energy to do. We are excited at the thought of you growing closer to God, growing closer to your group, and growing closer to a vision for your life through the Going Deeper section. Enjoy!

—SCOTT REALL, Director of Restore Ministries,
a life-changing ministry of the YMCA

STARTING YOUR
JOURNEY TO FREEDOM

YOUR LIFE SO FAR

Luther Gulick was the physical education instructor at the YMCA training school in Springfield, Massachusetts. In December 1891, he stood at his office window and looked across the school grounds covered with a blanket of decaying autumn leaves. Bare trees shivered in the north wind, and Gulick knew that the eighteen rugby-loving men that he would be in charge of over the winter would despise his indoor games. They hated the games of Leapfrog and Drop the Handkerchief. They were tired of tumbling inside while snow fell on icy creeks. They needed stimulation, something to keep them from going stir-crazy.

So Gulick challenged James Naismith and other physical education instructors to develop new indoor games. He gave them two weeks, which would be a daunting task, but Naismith jumped at the challenge and tried combinations of several games, mixing and matching them. Nothing seemed to work. Then he remembered a rock-throwing game that he'd played in childhood. Maybe he could come up with some variation of it. He doodled out a diagram, placing two goals at each end of the running track. He felt that he might have something, so he quickly summoned the school janitor and asked for two boxes. He was going to fasten each box at opposite ends of the running track.

But the janitor couldn't find boxes and brought back two half-bushel peach baskets. Naismith decided that this would have to do, and the janitor secured them at opposite ends. Then he divided the eighteen men into two teams and tacked thirteen rules to the wall. After each goal, the janitor lugged out the ladder and retrieved the ball. This is how the staff at the YMCA invented basketball.

SPIRIT

"The men where you live," said the little prince, "raised five thousand roses in the same garden—and they do not find in it what they are looking for." "They do not find it?" I replied. "And yet what they are looking for could be found in one single rose or in a little water." "Yes, that is true," I said, and the little prince added: "But the eyes are blind. One must look with the heart. . . ."

—ANTOINE DE SAINT-EXPUÉRY, *THE LITTLE PRINCE*

Luther Gulick and James Naismith believed in the possibility of new indoor games. They focused on the solution instead of the problem. The first goal on the journey to freedom is to believe in the possibility of change. Everyone has the potential to secure a lifetime of hope, health, and happiness. Change is available to everyone. The future can be different.

Maybe you are staring into a difficult situation. Maybe you feel like a bare tree shivering in the winter of discontent. Like Gulick, you know that something needs to change. But the journey to freedom can be confusing. There are so many remedies and philosophies of change. How do you find the one that's right for you?

The first stage of finding the right program or philosophy is pre-contemplation. You need to know where to apply the process of change. Maybe you need to lose weight or change jobs or stop being an approval addict. Maybe you need to overcome regret. Perhaps you've hit a dead end and you are completely confused. You only know that something needs to change. This is okay—pre-contemplation is the spadework.

But pre-contemplation of change cannot happen unless we first believe in the possibility of change.

ANGEL IN THE STONE

One day Pope Julius II watched Michelangelo hammering away at a slab of marble. "Why are you working so hard?" he asked. Michelangelo replied, "Can't you see there's an angel imprisoned in this block of stone? I'm working as hard as I can to set him free."

Inside us is the person that we were meant to be. We only need to chip away the parts that keep us in bondage to fear, to addictions, to low self-esteem, to feeling unworthy to be loved by God and others. Change is what happens when we break free from these hindrances.

But we have to believe in the possibility of change before we can be set free. Your interest in this book is evidence that you desire change. Somewhere inside, possibility still exists. This is a good thing. You are going to be okay. Change is possible. See yourself as stone and God as the sculptor who is working to set you free. We only need to remain still and let God chip some things away. Yes, it will be painful. Yes, it will be difficult. Unlike the stone, we will feel it. But we have to trust the process.

We have to ask tough questions: "What holds me in bondage? What areas of my life need change? Why do I feel hopeless?" These questions will arise during the process of change, but don't feel broken beyond repair. Psychiatrist and spiritual counselor Gerald May says that, when we fail at managing ourselves, we feel defective.[1] We all feel like this at times, but it shouldn't hold us back from believing in the possibility of change.

The Israelites stood before the Red Sea with Pharaoh closing fast behind them, trapping them between the two. Moses said to the Israelites, "Don't be afraid! Stand still. . . . You only need to remain calm; the LORD will fight for you" (Exod. 14:13–14). The possibility of victory was the first thing that God communicated to them. He wanted them to know that freedom was available. To be still and wait in the present requires hope and a sense of promise for the future. This is the essence of change. Possibility abounds.

The second goal on the journey to freedom is to realize that we need help. Gulick recognized the possibilities of change, and this led to Naismith's invention of basketball. Our belief in possibility can lead us to the One who can invent change in our life. Saint Augustine once said that God is always trying to give good things to us, but our hands are too full to receive them. Put another way, God is always trying to produce change in us, but we can't stop worrying long enough to receive it.

Worry is the enemy of change. We worry that we will not be able to change. We worry about not being worthy of change. We worry that change will broadcast our faults to the world. But as long as we are in bondage to worry, we will never reach out for the possibility of change. Gulick did not despair over the state of the eighteen men whom he'd have to play Drop the Handkerchief with that winter. He focused on finding an answer to the problem. Instead of worrying himself into despair, he cleared his mind, so he could do as Oswald Chambers said: "Let God's truth work in you by soaking in it, not by worrying into it. Obey God in the thing He is at present showing you, and instantly the next thing is opened up."[2]

This seems to be how it happened for Luther Gulick and James Naismith. They believed in the possibility of change, and they did what God was showing them in the moment. For Gulick it was to commission physical education instructors to come up with new game ideas. He needed outside help. Sometimes it takes others to get us further on the journey to freedom.

Freedom is found in numbers: "An enemy might defeat one person, but two people together can defend themselves; a rope that is woven of three strings is hard to break" (Eccles. 4:12). Those who bind themselves together conquer foes, because two are better than one. And when everything within us says, "You can do this alone," be careful. Secrecy is enslavement, and if enslavement is the result of doing it alone, let's tell someone so that we can be free. We can overthrow secret thoughts of despair, destruction, and addiction—but we have to come out of hiding. We need true friends. We need the help of others.

The third goal on the journey to freedom is to make the process of change concrete instead of a theory. There are many who can talk the theory of change, but somewhere change has to be made in concrete steps. Gulick wanted indoor games to change, so he took a concrete step and challenged those around him to invent new ones. This is pre-contemplation at the beginning of the journey.

We must consider whether we want to take concrete steps toward change. Christ asked the same question of the paralyzed man at the Pool of Bethesda. He asked, "Do you want to be made well?" (John 5:6 NKJV). He did not doubt the man's sincerity. He'd been lying by the pool for thirty-eight years. The paralytic man thought that he wanted to be made well, but Christ was asking something different. In essence He was saying, "A healing will change your life. You will have to get a job to support yourself. You will have to learn a new way of life." Christ was not questioning the theory of healing, but the concrete steps that he'd have to take to enjoy his freedom. At some point, healing and growth require concrete steps. This is the opportunity set before you. This has been your life so far, but it can change. Look upon the next six weeks as a challenge.

Gulick challenged Naismith to invent new games; your challenge is to come up with a new game plan for your life. The journey to a lifetime of hope, health, and happiness begins when we say, "I want to change. I want to be made well."

REFLECTIONS

CHANGING OUR LIVES BEGINS BY FIRST
BELIEVING THAT CHANGE IS POSSIBLE.

1. What does hope mean to you?

2. If you could change anything in your life, what would it be?

3. How long have you been thinking about changing your life?

4. How would you respond if Christ asked you personally, "Do you want to be made well?"

GOING DEEPER . . .

Read John 5:1–15 to learn the full story of the man who wanted to be healed and how he was made well.

THE LIFE THAT YOU WANT

The students at the YMCA training school in Springfield, Massachusetts, loved basketball so much that they took it back to their hometowns during Christmas break, and the game began to spread like wildfire. On January 15, 1892, Naismith published the first official basketball rules, and an indoor winter sport was born. Women quickly picked up the game—local schoolteachers were the first to play. The first "official" women's team was formed a year later, with Naismith's future wife among the players. With this kind of phenomenal growth came changes.

When we think about basketball today, we think of dunking; we think of Michael Jordan as he double-clutches the ball and slams it home. We think of the three-point line and zone defense. We think of March Madness and the NBA playoffs. But in the beginning, basketball was rugged, with inept rugby players who had to learn a different type of ball handling. And for the life of them, they couldn't remember the thirteen rules that Naismith posted on the wall. We can picture all eighteen men, plus Naismith and the janitor, huddled around the thirteen rules, trying to deal with a dispute. Probably some of the men questioned a foul or the way someone was handling the ball. Knowing human nature as we do, some may have felt that they could come up with better rules.

But if we could have attended the very first basketball game, we would have noticed their lack of ability. They weren't very good. A high-school junior-varsity team would have given those eighteen men a run for their money. The first game consisted of two fifteen-minute halves with five minutes of rest between, and ended with the score of 1–0. They stunk. They needed practice, and they needed to learn the rules.

So it is with all of us who attempt change. In the beginning, we'll stink. We'll need practice. We'll take one step forward and two steps back. The harder we try, it will seem, the harder change becomes. Expect this. No one masters their problem areas overnight. "No one ever saw a country begin in one day; no one has ever heard of a new nation beginning in one moment" (Isa. 66:8). We must never demand "overnight delivery" of ourselves. We are not a package headed for Pittsburgh. We are on a journey to freedom. It takes discipline and trial and error. So keep this in mind. Give yourself room to fail.

Annie Dillard writes that the life expectancy of a crop-duster pilot is five years. "They fly too low. They hit buildings and power lines. They have no space to fly out of trouble, and no space to recover from a stall."[1] Give yourself room to stall and space to recover. It may take a while to see the results of change.

It will take some time to reap the benefits of change. Nothing grows overnight. If you don't feel as though you are reaping any benefits, give it some time. Make a spacious place for God to work when you stall. This way you will never crash because, just as the life expectancy of a crop duster is five years, the dropout rate of most programs of change is around 50 percent. To keep yourself out of this statistic, leave space for God to work. Don't give up. Change never happens as fast as we'd like. We have to learn the steps, just as the first basketball team had to refer to their rules, so keep coming back to this simple rule: Change, recovery, growth, and healing are all about hope.

Hope is a fundamental part of change. Henri Nouwen writes, "Hope is trusting that something will be fulfilled, but fulfilled according to the promises and not just according to our wishes. Therefore hope is always open ended."[2] Hope believes in spite of the circumstances. Hope is open to change. It is not dedicated to doing the same things over and over again with the same old results. Hope thinks new thoughts.

THE BOTTOM OF THE PEACH BASKETS

In the beginning of basketball, when someone scored a goal, the janitor climbed the ladder, retrieved the ball from the basket, and threw it to a player. Then they carted the ladder off the court. But as the accuracy of the players increased, so did the number of times that the janitors had to retrieve the ball. Then someone got the ingenious idea of cutting the bottoms out of the peach baskets. This revolutionized the game. They tried something different in hopes of making the game more efficient. Eventually, metal rims and cord nets replaced the baskets.

The first goal for today is to concentrate on making life better, not perfect. Avoid the idea that change is a matter of perfection. We are learning new principles to live by, which means that we need patience. The reason people drop out of a program of change is that they feel like permanent failures. But remember that mistakes are not fatal. Problems are only temporary. Circumstances change.

Start a journal. Write down the negative things that you worry will come true. Then go back in six weeks and see how many of them actually took place. Begin to concentrate more on how things can change, instead of worrying about how bad things are.

The second goal for today is to understand the presence of a crisis. Usually we don't change until our problems cause a crisis. For the game of basketball, it was the crisis of wasted time retrieving the ball. In our lives, we begin the process of change when life becomes unmanageable. Our problems dominate our time and energy. We get tired. We reach the point that we just can't face another day of pain. As C. S. Lewis said, pain is God's megaphone. It is a shipwreck of our own making. And to get back to the surface, we must suffer the consequences of our actions.

We do this by refusing to involve loved ones. We stop blaming others. We no longer manipulate other people for selfish gain. We cease to run. We face our crisis and take responsibility for it. Thomas Merton called this the "darkness of the beginning."[3] We become overwhelmed and, in a sense, fall to our knees. We cry out for help from the blackest hole. It's the moment when we cut the bottom out of our peach basket problems, making way for a revolution in our lives.

MIND

You need to claim the events of your life to make yourself yours.
—ANN WILSON SCHAEF

When all of our human resources and efforts fail us, we tend to empty our hands so that God can fill them with Himself. This happened to me after I suffered through a divorce. I'd reached the end of myself. I struggled with low self-esteem because I felt like a failure. I could not fill the hole in my heart. I'd tried acquiring worldly possessions. I pursued power. I sought human relationships. I tried sports. I tried writing screenplays and pursued different jobs. Nothing seemed to help. I believed that perhaps a new relationship with a woman could fix me and make me complete so that I would feel good about myself again. I felt hopeless. "I will never change," I told myself. "This is all I will ever know."

Then it was as if God called to me, and the only thing I could think to do was get in my car and drive to Percy Warner Park in Nashville, Tennessee. I've always felt close to God in nature, and I knew I had to get alone with Him. It was fall, and the trees of Tennessee were on fire with dashes of orange and red and the yellows of diminishing green leaves. I parked my car and made my way beneath oaks and ashes, hackberries, locusts, and maples. I heard nothing and saw no one but the leaves as they began their descent, glancing ever so gently off those that remained on the trees. The air was full of them and the ground was blanketed. They crackled beneath my feet as I walked deeper into the woods, searching for a place to collapse on my knees. It was my "darkness of the beginning," the place where I finally cried out to God about the hole in my life. I wanted to be made well. In the midst of nature's changing season, I fell to my knees and cried for six hours, until nothing remained. It was the beginning of a new life for me.

After that day in the park, I got into a twelve-step program and began the most difficult part of change—self-examination. It was the moment when I cut out the bottom of my peach basket. I tried something different. The same old thing with the same old results had to change, so I stopped looking for fulfillment in a relationship with another person. I learned to love God and be loved by God. Whether we know it or not, this is what we all desire. I discovered this in the presence of my crisis.

The third goal for today is knowing where to place the X. Clifton Fadiman tells a story about Charles Steinmetz, an electrical engineer genius who worked for General Electric in the early part of the twentieth century. After his retirement, they called him in because the other engineers were baffled about the breakdown of a complex of machines. They asked Steinmatz to pinpoint the problem. He walked around the machines for a while, then took a piece of chalk out of his pocket and made a big cross mark on one particular machine. When the engineers disassembled that part of the machine, it turned out to be the precise location of the breakdown.

A few days later, the engineers received a bill from Steinmatz for $10,000— a staggering sum in those days. They asked him to itemize it, and he returned the bill with a note that read:

Making one cross mark: $1
Knowing where to put it: $9,999[4]

Changing our lives always starts with putting the cross mark on the right spot. This is the work of pre-contemplation. Gerald May writes, "How much can I respect myself if I do not even know what I really want?"[5] I'll add, "How can I change if I haven't identified the problem?" Pre-contemplation is learning where to look for the problem. A weight problem may be the result of emotional eating due to some overwhelming hurt. An addiction problem may be the result of a deep-seated insecurity. Until we perform a self-examination, we will not have a clue about how to change.

My guess is that this is the reason why most people drop out of groups. Either they feel broken beyond repair, or they don't know why their life is broken. They can point to many things that are wrong, but they do not know where to draw the X. We need outside help. Other people can help us find the spot if we are willing to look. Looking is the key.

This is what Luther Gulick did when he stood at his window that day in 1891. He thought about the eighteen rugby-loving men who did not want to play Drop the Handkerchief. He didn't place the mark on their chests, blaming them for their dissatisfaction. He placed the mark on the fact that the current indoor games were not meeting their needs. He then took the crisis and changed the face of indoor games with the help of James Naismith.

The presence of a crisis may be the beginning of a new life. God loves to redeem shattered lives. He's the source of power to help us on the journey to freedom.

REFLECTIONS

HOPE IS A FUNDAMENTAL PART OF CHANGE.

1. When have you lost all hope of changing? Share about that time in your life.

2. If someone instructed you to mark an X on each part of your life that is broken, where would you put the X?

3. Describe a time when you have been most willing to surrender to God.

GOING DEEPER . . .

Read Philippians 3:12–14 to see where the apostle Paul admits his own lack of perfection.

FINDING HOPE

One of James Naismith's former students, Phog Allen, is considered the "father of basketball coaching." Allen told Naismith that he was going to Baker University to coach basketball. Naismith said, "Why, basketball is just a game to play. It doesn't need a coach." But the University of Kansas counts Naismith among its coaches. Evidently, he changed his mind about a coaching career and coached basketball there for nine years.

The inventor of the game is the only coach in University of Kansas history with a losing record: fifty-three wins and fifty-five losses. The man who invented basketball could not coach his way to a winning record. But to see Naismith as a basketball failure would be a gross injustice. He invented it, so his losing record only makes him human. He is a great example of how we live with the tension of both failures and successes.

Everyone has failures. If we don't win at certain things, it doesn't mean that we are permanent failures. We may win next time, or we may lose three more times before we win. But the trap that most of us fall into is what psychologists call disqualifying the positive—that is, drawing conclusions from only the negative. Naismith could have thought of himself as a failure because of his losing record. But this would have disqualified his positive contribution of inventing basketball.

Everyone has positive things of worth in their lives. Our jobs may be unrewarding, but our children may bring us much joy. To focus only on the negative aspects of our careers is to disqualify the joy of having children. Our financial circumstances may be challenged, but our marriages may be great. To focus only on the finances disqualifies a great relationship. The moment that we allow the negatives to ruin the positives, life gets out of balance. Relationships end in turmoil; jobs become drudgery.

We are never without hope. We can never disqualify God's help. He offers the great possibility of life. The Bible says, "We know that in everything God works for the good of those who love him."[1] God will take bad things and bring something good from them. This is the hope that we are looking for—the hope of God's help. Remember, Augustine said that God is always trying to give good things to us, but our hands are often too full to receive them. This is what it means to disqualify God's help. There are times when we believe that life is manageable on our own, so we stick to what we think is working. But in reality, each day moves us closer and closer toward becoming a negative person who gives up on life.

C. S. Lewis deals with the differences between heaven and hell in his book *The Great Divorce*. In this fictional piece, people from earth take a day trip to the bright borders of heaven, where they seem to become ghosts against the brilliance of that place. The narrator embarks on an incredible voyage through heaven and hell, meeting a host of supernatural beings that teach him the nature of good and evil. One ghost wanders into the narrator's path with a little red lizard on his shoulder. The lizard whips its tail back and forth while whispering lustful words into the ghost's ear, tormenting him with thoughts of evil. An angel offers to kill the lizard, but the ghost says, "Honestly, I don't think there's the slightest necessity for that. I'm sure I shall be able to keep it in order now."[2]

BODY

Strength training is the fountain of youth. It maintains or increases our lean muscle mass, which permanently raises our rested metabolic rate, the amount of calories we burn at rest; it maintains or increases our bone mass and helps prevent osteoporosis.

SPIRIT

> When a man is at his wits' end, it is not a cowardly thing to pray; it is the only way he can get in touch with reality.
>
> —OSWALD CHAMBERS, *MY UTMOST FOR HIS HIGHEST*

It seems rational for us to believe that we can keep our own lives in order, just as the ghost in Lewis's story believed that he could keep the red lizard in order. Sometimes we can keep our own "lizards" at bay. Sometimes we feel as if we are free of them. But then the whispers begin again. The trap that we fall into is trying to maintain the normality of a life that isn't working. We believe that we can handle our problems on our own. This is the lie of normality.

The first goal of the day is to end normality. We have to admit that the life we are now leading isn't working. Decide to switch from mere survival to a new way of life.

A recent television program showed a method for trapping monkeys. The natives made a hole in a log and put bait inside. The hole was just big enough to allow the monkey room to get his opened hand inside the log. The monkey reached his hand in to get the bait, but when his fingers closed on it he couldn't get his fist back through the hole. The monkey was determined to hang on to what he had, and soon he was captured, trapped by his own greed. We are much like this monkey when we hold on to a life of normality. We fail to do the one thing that would free us, which is to let go and try a new way of life.

The second goal of the day is to identify the traits of our normality so we can begin to eliminate them. Think about the areas of your life that need change. This means even the areas that you may think you are managing with normality.

In Day 2, we discussed how our problems are temporary. Now we begin the process of listing the areas where we desire change. This is not an action step, but merely a way to get you to think through what can or cannot change in your life. So, take a few minutes and list your problem areas.

The areas in which I desire change are:

1. _____

2. _____

3. _____

4. _____

5. _____

Once you've listed these areas, begin to think about some areas that will never change. Unchangeable areas need pinpointing in the pre-contemplation stage. This way you will not get frustrated and quit with all-or-nothing thinking, which is the belief that our life has to be perfect in every area or it is a failure. Keep in mind that many areas can change for the better, but life will not be a work of perfection. Make peace with this before you begin the journey to freedom. This is the thought behind the Serenity Prayer:

God grant me the serenity to accept the things I cannot change; courage to change the things I can; and wisdom to know the difference—living one day at a time, one moment at a time; accepting hardships as a pathway to peace; taking as Jesus did, this sinful world as it is, not as I would have it; trusting that You will make all

things right which I surrender to Your will, so that I may be rea-
sonably happy in this life and supremely happy with You forever
in the next. Amen.

—Reinhold Niebuhr

The wisdom to know the difference is the key. Focus on what can
change. Many times we become obsessed with things over which we
have no control, such as other people. We cannot control their behavior
and make them treat us nicely. We can also blame our circumstances on
others. It's easy to say that we've tried it all and nothing has worked, and
we refuse to give our circumstances a new look.

This happened to Jesus' disciples. They had fished all night on the
Lake of Galilee and caught nothing. Early the next morning, Jesus stood
on the shore and called out to them, "Friends, did you catch any fish?"
They answered, "No." He said, "Throw your net on the right side of the
boat, and you will find some." So they did, and they caught so many fish
that they could not pull the net back into the boat.[3]

The disciples were fishermen by trade. They knew the lake. They
knew the shoreline and the depths. They knew all about fishing—what
worked and what didn't. But they failed to do one thing: they failed to
see the trap of normality.

Jesus didn't order them to park the boat and take up a rod and reel. He
didn't force them into doing something that contradicted their knowledge of fishing. He only suggested another style—the other side of the
boat. This is the God factor. An old fishing hole becomes a full net.
Attain new heights with God's help. Remain open. If you feel shoved
into change, you will disqualify the positive and quit.

The goal is to make life better, not perfect. Fight normality, which is
the fear of living in a different way. If Naismith feared change, then
today's basketball retrieval method would still be climbing a ladder. He
could have said, "This is how we play the game. There is no other way."
But he was flexible and open to trying something different if it improved
the game. This is the decision that we make in pre-contemplation. We

open our minds to a new kind of life. We make the commitment to think in new ways to improve life.

The third goal of the day is to discover a vision. On Day 2, I told the story of reaching the end of myself at Percy Warner Park. In that moment, everything was dark. I had no vision. I was too deep in the blackness to see my way out of my circumstances. I needed God's help. It was the "darkness of the beginning." And the important word here is *beginning.* The darkness may have been great in the beginning, but now we need the light. We need vision.

In pre-contemplation, we find the vision that is the opposite of the world's—the opposite of obtaining wealth, power, and prestige. Society believes that happiness is a result of these three things. I thought that one more relationship would make me complete, but it never did. I found myself exhausted and hopeless. We need to begin to think about where we want life to take us from here. This is vision. It's a simple goal, done one day at a time. And the goal of every day is to trust at all times that God is with you and will meet your needs. Finding hope is a matter of trust.

When the disciples were done fishing on the other side of the boat, they found hot coals and fish already on the fire when they reached the shore. Jesus provided breakfast. He had a plan for their day. And the key to hope is to believe every day that Jesus will appear with the resources that you need to walk out the new life that He calls you to live. Christ's presence brings success. Stay close to Him, and He will bring the power that you need. He knows how to guide you. He knows where the fish are located. He sees all things. The Bible says, "When you pass through the waters, I will be with you. When you cross rivers, you will not drown. When you walk through fire, you will not be burned, nor will the flames hurt you."[4]

Finding hope involves making new decisions about our old way of life. It's about God's presence on the journey. As Saint Teresa of Avila said, "The feeling remains that God is on the journey, too."

REFLECTIONS

THE MOMENT THAT WE ALLOW THE NEGATIVES TO
RUIN THE POSITIVES, OUR LIVES GET OUT OF BALANCE.

1. Like the monkey, have you ever felt trapped by something you could not let go of? What are some of the things in your life that you feel trapped by?

2. Why do we have a hard time letting go of some things, even when we know they are bad for our lives?

3. How have you experienced God's presence in your life during difficult times?

GOING DEEPER . . .

*Read Isaiah 43:1–7 and 18–19 to see how God is always present in our lives,
even during our trials.*

REAL CHANGE OCCURS IN THREE AREAS

In 1893, basketball developed a huge problem. Overzealous spectators in the balcony were interfering with the game. They'd reach down and knock the ball away from the basket, infuriating the players and endangering the fairness of the game. Something had to be done about the interference. But what? They could not move the spectators out of the balcony or reposition the goals. The search for a remedy soon led to the creation of the first backboard, which was made out of wire mesh. And it worked! The backboard defended the goal against the spectators who were impeding the game.

One of the things that we will face while trying to change our lives is interference. Numerous self-defeating behaviors can interfere with our process of change. We can undervalue ourselves and be unaware of our inadequacies or the life skills that we possess to overcome them. But knowledge can raise awareness and build a safety net of protection against these self-defeating behaviors, just as the game of basketball used the backboard to defend the goal from interference. Energy that we expend against ourselves will weaken our power to change. It interferes with success.

THREE INTERFERENCE ATTITUDES

There are three interference attitudes that will impede our attempts change. "I tried it once, and it didn't work." Many of us attempt change, only to give up after one try. We believe that we are what we are and can never change. We try to quit smoking and fail after only one day. We tell ourselves that we don't have what it takes. We tell ourselves that it's impossible. We go on a diet, but after a week of failing to lose any significant weight, we say, "I can't lose weight. There's nothing I can do about it." Others try harder, believing that willpower can change them, but soon that, too, fails.

Willpower is an element of change, but it is not the deciding factor. The way to overcome the self-defeating behavior of giving up is to *train*, not to *try*. Training versus trying is the key to success. John Ortberg writes, "Spiritual transformation is not a matter of trying harder, but of training wisely. . . . There is an immense difference between training to do something and trying to do something."[1] When we try to change and do not succeed, we tend to give up after a few attempts. But when we train to do something, we set our minds on learning. No matter how many times we fail, we see ourselves as being one step closer to succeeding.

An Olympic athlete doesn't just show up and try really hard on the day of a particular event. He trains his spirit, mind, and body long before the Olympics even begin. You may not be an Olympian, but training is the key to reaching every goal. A weight lifter progresses toward his goal by training his muscles a little at a time. If he fails, he trains his muscles until they exert the power needed to reach the desired goal. Ortberg writes, "Trying hard can accomplish only so much . . . you will have to enter into a life of training."[2] Trying is the raw use of willpower, nothing more. Training is learning the life skills needed for long-term change.

Start where you are with the mind-set of training your spirit, mind, and body over the next thirty-six days. Allow your spirit to be inspired. Learn health tips. Raise the awareness of your mind, so you can train for freedom. This is the success that Phil discovered at Restore.

Phil first came to Restore Ministries at the YMCA because he'd tried hard to change with willpower and failed. Multiple drunk-driving incidents and an accident landed him in jail for a year, and during all of this turmoil, he lost his home, business, and fiancée. To make it worse, after being released from jail, he soon was stopped again for drunk driving. This is when Phil hit rock bottom. He came to the realization that alcohol was his downfall. But he wasn't sure whether another recovery program would help. He'd tried numerous programs and failed. Instead of training and learning from his mistakes, he plunged deeper into a vortex of darkness as he continued to try harder, only to fail. Nothing seemed to work. He felt that he would never change.

At Restore, Phil learned that lasting change takes place when we bring into harmony the spirit, mind, and body. And once we helped Phil plug into the spiritual dimension, he was transformed. His mind had been divided from his body and spirit, and as long as this was taking place he could not change. Gerald May believes that maintaining a healthy balance between the spirit, mind, and body is how we change. He writes, "Both Eastern and Western medical sciences have long understood that maintaining natural balances is the body's greatest priority; if the systems of the body are going to work at all, they must work together in harmony. When equilibrium is thrown off balance, the result is stress."[3]

SPIRIT

"It is worth nothing for them to have the whole world if they lose their souls."
—MATTHEW 16:26

The key in the process of lasting change is to balance the spirit, mind, and body. This has been the YMCA's focus for over a hundred years. The YMCA knew early on that, even though a person might be a physical specimen of robust health, his spirit may be malnourished, and before long there is a disconnection. In Phil's case, he had medicated his mind, but he'd damaged his body and spirit. Anytime we leave out one of the three, it produces stress in the body, low self-esteem in the mind, and displacement in the spirit. It causes us to long for the wrong objects—power, prestige, and possessions.

DISQUALIFYING THE POSITIVE

The backboard defended the game of basketball from overzealous spectators, and it revolutionized the game on the court, turning a negative into a positive. Players learned to shoot using the backboard. We often hear people at a basketball game yell, "Use the board." Now this is good advice, but in 1893, the backboard had only one function—to stop the interference. Later, the players discovered that the backboard had multiple positives. It helped their shots and propelled the game forward to become what it is today.

SPIRIT

I saw the angel in stone and carved until I set him free.
—MICHELANGELO

Every situation has a positive element to it that can lead to change. The way to overcome negative interference is by eliminating what has been called the "yeah, but" syndrome. Let's say your boss gives you the promotion that you've longed for, and someone congratulates you—but you say, "Yeah, but it means that I'll have more responsibilities." Or maybe you lose twenty pounds and someone pays you a compliment, and you respond, "Yeah, but I'm not at the weight I was in high school." You may never get back to your high school weight, so don't disqualify the progress that you've made or injure the positive. Any energy that we expend disqualifying the positive takes away from our power to change. It interferes with success.

Martin Seligman, professor of psychology at the University of Pennsylvania, writes: "Finding temporary and specific causes for misfortune is the art of hope. People who make permanent and universal explanations for their troubles tend to collapse under pressure, both for a long time and across situations."[4] So hope is an integral part of change. If James Naismith had allowed the overzealous spectators to take over the game, their actions could have permanently injured the game. But he saw it as a temporary setback that needed a solution, not a detrimental blow to the game of basketball.

Maybe you've hit an obstacle. Something is interfering with your hope, health, or happiness. Is it a temporary setback or a permanent one? If you interpret it as a temporary hindrance, you can discover ways, as Phil did, to overcome it. But if you disqualify the positive, you may feel helpless and hopeless. You may remain stuck in a pattern of defeat. The awareness you can raise is to understand that your problems are temporary. You can overcome them.

APPROVAL ADDICTION

The third interference is "approval addiction." Everyone desires love and acceptance, but when we search for fulfillment in all the wrong relationships, it can disconnect our spirit from God. Dr. Gerald May writes, "All human beings have an inborn desire for God. Whether we are consciously religious or not, this desire is our deepest longing and our most precious treasure. It gives us meaning."[5]

The way to block the interference of seeking approval at all costs is to see it for what it is: a need for love and a desire for God, the source of all love and acceptance. Without God's love, it feels as if there is a hole in our soul where life leaks out. We frantically seek to fill this hole with objects of desire, such as addictions, bad relationships, impulsive behavior, and other things that ultimately don't satisfy our craving for God's love. I spent almost my entire life running to different objects. Now I understand the hard truth that I entered every area of life with an emotional deficit. It was here in total isolation that I felt hopeless. I longed for someone to love and accept me so that I could feel good about myself. But no human or substance can fill the God-sized hole in our soul.

MIND

The life which is not examined is not worth living.
—PLATO

In the movie *The Last Samurai*, Nathan Algren provides a great example of a man with a hole in his soul. He had regrets. He wished that he could change the horrors of war that haunted him, because somewhere on the unforgiving plains near the banks of the Washita River, Algren's soul was wounded. He became an empty cup with a hole. No matter how hard he tried to fill it with alcohol, it didn't seal the hole. While held captive in a Samurai village, he became severely ill as a result of alcohol withdrawal. He told the Samurai leader that he didn't care if he lived or died. But during his captivity he was awakened to the hole in his soul and went through a spiritual transformation.

We seek today what Nathan Algren sought—something that will make us feel alive again, something to seal the hole in our soul. Phil's drinking never cured his emptiness or set him free. Addictions never fulfill our longings to love and be loved. Turning to God and trusting Him seals the hole. Then He helps us learn to balance the spirit, mind, and body in such a way that they no longer interfere with one another, but complement each other's growth.

Phil plugged into the spiritual dimension and moved from bondage to freedom. Maybe you need to integrate the exercise of the body into your life to get the change that you seek. Or maybe you need to integrate the right thoughts by refusing to give up, and by rejecting the impulse to disqualify the positive. Maybe you have a hole in your soul and the desire to love and be loved by God. Whatever the case, real change occurs in three areas: spirit, mind, and body. When we train in all three areas, the training propels the process of change.

REFLECTIONS

THE KEY TO THE PROCESS OF CHANGE IS TO BALANCE OUR SPIRIT, MIND, AND BODY.

1. What might be a first step for you to grow in spirit?

In body?

In mind?

2. What do you see as the critical difference between *trying to change* and *training for change*? In what areas do you *try* and in what areas do you *train*?

3. Why do addictions never fulfill our longings to love and to be loved? How has this been true in your life?

GOING DEEPER . . .

Read I Corinthians 9:24–27 and consider the importance of training your body, mind, and spirit.

THE GIFT OF FEELINGS

The movie *Ordinary People* has the best portrayal of what happens when we do not allow ourselves to feel our true feelings. The movie is a stark reality about a younger brother, Conrad, living in the aftermath of his older, more loved brother's death. Throughout the movie, we see Conrad running away from his feelings, trying not to feel the pain of his brother's accidental death that has left him plagued with shame and guilt. Conrad begins counseling with a therapist, Dr. Berger, because he has attempted suicide in order to escape the pain. After a sequence of events, including a friend's suicide, Conrad has a flood of feelings that frightens him and forces him to once again revisit feelings and emotions that he had suppressed long ago.

MIND

Imagination is an internal focus on the desires of the heart that lead to full living. It is courageous willingness to make the visions of the heart's desires our highest goal. Imagination includes the knowledge that we may have pain in obtaining our desires, but ultimately our desires are more powerful than our pain.

—DR. CHIP DODD, *VOICE OF THE HEART*

Those feelings brought him to a place of contemplating suicide instead of feeling the pain. In his pain and confusion he reaches out to Dr. Berger for help. At the end, Dr. Berger finally gets Conrad to open up about where the hurt in his life actually began. Conrad talks for the first time about the day his brother drowned. He finally broke down and let the feelings pour out because Dr. Berger pushed him even further to truly feel the pain that he had been hiding for so many years. Conrad finally begins to embrace those feelings and Dr. Berger says, "Feelings are scary. And sometimes they're painful. And if you can't feel pain . . . you won't feel anything else either." This was the beginning of his healing and true recovery.

SPIRIT

To have shame as an identity is to believe that one's being is flawed, that one is defective as a human being. Once shame is transformed into an identity, it becomes toxic.
—JOHN BRADSHAW, *HEALING THE SHAME THAT BINDS YOU*

We all struggle with feelings on a daily basis. Most of us are afraid to feel our feelings because of what we think it means or what might happen. We also have been taught that some feelings are bad and we shouldn't feel them. Feelings are not bad; it is the actions that sometimes result when we experience an impaired version of a feeling that can be bad. If we don't understand the purpose or functions of our feelings, we could end up like Conrad in the movie *Ordinary People*, stuffing our feelings into self-destructive outlets and into other addictions. They can push us into states of depression, anxiety, isolation, and confusion.

I did the same things. When I would feel sadness, fear, or loneliness, I would want to medicate. For years when I was struggling with addictions, at the core of those addictions were incredible feelings of loneliness and sadness. I was terrified to admit that to anyone. Usually on the weekends, these feelings would rear their ugly heads. The weekend is a very difficult time for a lot of people because you are always being asked on Friday at work, "So what are you doing this weekend?" When you don't have an exciting answer, those feelings are bound to come pouring out. I dreaded the expectations of specific dates such as holidays, anniversaries, birthdays, or anything of that nature because they would make those feelings come back again.

I would medicate on those days so I would not have to feel those feelings—because those feelings brought such discomfort for me. When I finally began my recovery, someone told me that if an addict has to choose between feeling pain and feeling nothing, the addict chooses to feel nothing. In recovery I do choose to feel my feelings; that means often having to feel pain. That pain will let me feel my feelings. I had to let them teach me, allow God to use them, and let me live from my heart and not use the various forms of avoidance that I was medicating with. We must learn not to avoid and escape our feelings. If we do we will miss the greatest gift that they can bring us: freedom.

Dr. Chip Dodd says, "Feelings are the voice of the heart. And you will not have fullness unless you are adept at hearing and experiencing all of them. When you are not aware of your feelings, your life is lived incompletely. Whenever you don't feel, you are blocked from living life to the fullest."[1]

Our journey to freedom must take us through our feelings. Our feelings must be embraced and be processed if we are to find freedom and fullness of life. When we avoid our feelings—by medicating, becoming depressed, or whatever that response is—we are going to stay stuck.

Dr. Dodd talks about eight feelings that we all experience in the human condition and how they help us purely experience and understand the depth of the heart. In the Journey to Freedom program, we have our participants name their feelings as a part of the healing process. There is power in identifying and understanding the eight feelings. They are: hurt, loneliness, sadness, anger, fear, shame, guilt, and gladness. Many people often look at this list and ask, "Why is only one feeling positive and all the others are negative?" The truth is that all eight feelings are good. Each feeling is positive because of where it can lead. Each feeling has it own specific purpose in helping us live life fully. Let's look at how each one benefits us on our journey.

Hurt leads to healing.

It is important that we identify what has hurt us. If I can identify that hurt, it will lead me to what is causing the pain, which will in turn guide me in the process of healing. Just think about when you go into a doctor's office: the first thing that he asks you is, "Where does it hurt?" He cannot give you an assessment or make you feel better until he knows what the problem is. It is the same with our pain. We cannot begin to heal until we admit that we were hurt. Then and only then can we deal with it. Dr. Dodd says, " For in the admission to hurt you also expose yourself to healing."[2]

Loneliness moves us to intimacy.

Loneliness exposes us to our hunger for relationships. If we will respond to loneliness in a healthy way, it will require us to take the initiative to be authentic with people. We will have to embrace the idea of being known and earnestly seek out relationships. God gave us this natural feeling so that we may use it to draw closer to Him, others, and ourselves.

Sadness expresses value and honor.

Sadness reveals how much we value something that we have lost. When my dog died, my world was turned upside down. I missed his unconditional love and the way that he was always there. I was profoundly sad at his passing because he meant so much to me. Sadness, if we will embrace it, reveals just how much we cared about something or someone. Sadness can show us just how valuable something was in our lives so that we might give it the honor that it deserves.

Anger hungers for life.

Anger lets my heart know that which really, truly matters to me. Anger can reveal how much my heart is affected by something that failed to happen. It can move us to go out and make a difference in our life and the lives of others. One of the best examples that I can think of is the first time that Jesus got really angry in the Bible. He came upon money changers making a mockery of God's holy place. Jesus expressed His great displeasure and cleared out those who were insulting all that He stood for. He saw what they were doing to such a precious and sacred place and He acted out of passion for His Father.[3] Anger shows how passionately something matters to us. It is the energy that can propel us to go out and do something that matters and truly make a difference.

Fear awakens us to danger and begins wisdom.

Fear is a healthy emotion in recovery. Let's take alcohol use for example. If I know that another drink can cause someone to be killed, that fear will awaken me to the many consequences that can happen from one simple act. Fear makes me see the dangerous possibilities of my actions and will guide me to wisdom in making future decisions. Fear can provide a sense of accountability and can motivate me to move in a direction toward recovery and healing. Healthy fear always leads to the beginning of wisdom.

Shame maintains humility and mercy.

Shame shows us that we cannot do everything, that we have limitations. It shows us that we are not God. Shame does not humiliate; it helps create humility within us. It should be a relief to know that we cannot and are not expected to do everything. Healthy shame leads me to identify that I am human, make mistakes, and need help.

Guilt brings forgiveness.

Guilt is what we feel when we do something wrong. It is all about behavior and actions. Guilt comes from actions that I did when I harmed someone or actions that I should have taken when I did not. If we listen to the guilt, we become aware of how we acted and know that we must make the situation or relationship right. Guilt leads me to seek forgiveness so relationships can be restored.

Gladness proves the hope of the heart to be true.

Gladness is the result of allowing ourselves to feel the other seven feelings. It is great to feel these feelings because it means that you and your heart are alive. If I will feel my feelings and live from my heart, then I will know true gladness.

If I am not living from my heart, then I am living from my addiction and I am not free to feel. Gladness comes from being free. Dr. Gerald May says that only a free heart is really alive.[4] That is what God wants. He does not want you bound, but free. All addictions that we have are about control. Hearts that are in bondage to the control of their feelings are not free. Where there is no freedom, there is no gladness.

BODY

If we wish to live the happy life, we have no choice but to exercise and become fit.

—DR. GEORGE SHEEHAN, *PERSONAL BEST*

The journey to freedom will require that we begin to live authentically from our hearts, where we embrace our feelings. Avoiding our feelings has become a way of life for many. It leads us to isolation and ultimately to different forms of medicating those feelings. These deeply ingrained patterns of avoiding our feelings begin to rule our lives by becoming life-controlling issues. To become free from these life-controlling issues, we must learn a new response to these feelings. That begins by understanding the tremendous value that God gave us through feelings. And as we learn to live from our hearts, feeling these feelings, we can begin the path to freedom.

IMPAIRMENT

When we think of feelings as negative, it is often because we have experienced what Dr. Dodd calls the "impaired" version of the feeling. This is what we experience when we don't allow ourselves to feel the true feeling. Just as each feeling has a "gift," each feeling has an impairment that comes when we do not allow ourselves to feel it.

Impaired Hurt: Resentment

Resentment is what happens when we try to avoid feeling hurt. Resentment deflects our focus away from our internal pain and on to someone or something else. Hurt most often comes in relationships, and God brings healing to where there has been hurt through relationships. He wants us to be vulnerable with Him about the relationship that is causing us pain. Only then can He heal our heart and move us forward.

Impaired Loneliness: Apathy

Apathy is the opposite of love. It says, "I just don't care anymore." If I refuse to feel loneliness, it will drive me inward even further into isolation and depression and possibly to other forms of self-medication. I can let my loneliness keep me from ever seeking out relationships and let it control my everyday activities for fear of letting people know me.

Impaired Sadness: Self-Pity

We often fear expressing sadness because we don't want to be seen as having self-pity. But in actuality true sadness and self-pity are very different. Dr. Dodd defines *self-pity* as "a way to escape the pain of sadness by trying to make others feel sadness for us."[5] If I am unwilling to feel sadness myself, I may try to get someone else to feel what I refuse to feel. This will not cleanse my heart and bring healing. I must allow myself to feel the depth of the loss and the sadness that comes from losing someone or something that I value.

Impaired Anger: Depression

Depression has often been defined as anger turned inward. It also occurs when I close off my desires and passions. The energy of anger is turned against myself, and I become worn out. I have no motivation, no energy, no passion—and no vision for my life. True anger is a good thing—it expresses our desire for life. This is different from how we may have thought about anger before, as uncontrollable rage. Rage is not an impairment of anger, but an impairment of fear.

Impaired Fear: Anxiety/Control/Rage:

Fear will drive us in one of two directions: it can drive us to faith and surrendering our lives to God's care, or it will drive us to try to control our circumstances in an attempt to avoid the negative event that we fear. Anxiety and worry are the result of not trusting God with our lives. When we are anxious, we will try to control the people and circumstances of our lives to conform to our expectations and needs. When they do not conform and we are unable to control them, we can react in rage. Rage destroys the benefit of fear because it is a refusal to face our fear of vulnerability to the point that it denies the fact that fear exists. Most people confuse rage and anger—we think that they are the same thing, when they really could not be further apart. Dr. Dodd puts it this way: "Rage rejects the fear of having desire. Anger is an acknowledgment of the depth of our desire."[6] This distinction can be crucial to our recovery. If you struggle with rage, the question that you need to ask yourself is not "what am I angry about?" but rather "what am I so afraid of?"

Impaired Shame: Toxic Shame

When I believe that I am flawed and defective as a human being, then I have moved away from a state of healthy shame and I constantly condemn and criticize myself. We call this toxic shame. It is where I have taken shame on as an identity—I am ashamed of who I am. It drives me to humiliation, which says "You are so bad," and away from my need for God and others.

Impaired Guilt: Pride/Toxic Shame

It is very dangerous when I do not feel guilt. If I do not feel remorse in my heart when I have done something wrong, then I will not seek forgiveness and relationships will remain fractured. Pride keeps us from asking for forgiveness because it rejects our true condition and refuses to be vulnerable to another person. In order not to feel guilt, we may blame others and justify our own actions so that we don't have to feel our own hurt. We can also go the other direction with guilt, and feel that we are not just guilty of a bad action—we are *all* bad. Toxic shame rejects the forgiveness of others and continues to feel bad even after we have sought forgiveness.

Impaired Gladness: Happiness/Entertainment

Happiness has its root in the word *happenstance*, which means that circumstances are what dictate our happiness. In an attempt to manufacture joy, we look to external events to bring us the happiness that we all desire. Yet haven't you found that those events never seem to quite fulfill our expectations? And we are left with a sense of wanting more. We may also try to find gladness through sensuous pleasure, such as sex, eating, sports, music, etc. While these can all be good things, they are temporary pleasures, which will not bring true, lasting fulfillment. If we are not finding fulfillment in feeling and owning all of our feelings in relationships, then these things end up being distractions that take us away from our heart rather than into our heart.

The Journey to Freedom will require that we begin to live authentically from our hearts where we embrace our feelings. Avoiding our feelings for many of us has become a way of life. It leads us to isolation and ultimately to different forms of medicating those feelings. These deeply ingrained patterns of avoiding our feelings begin to rule our lives by becoming life-controlling issues. To become free from these life-controlling issues, we must learn a new response to these feelings. That begins by understanding the tremendous value that God gave us through these feelings. And as we learn to live from our hearts, feeling these feelings, we can begin the path to freedom.

REFLECTIONS

LIFE IS NOT A CONSTANT EMERGENCY, BUT WHEN WE LIVE BY OUR EMOTIONS, EVERYTHING SEEMS LIKE AN EMOTIONAL EMERGENCY.

1. What feelings have you been avoiding or suppressing because you are afraid of the pain that comes with them?

2. How can we allow our feelings to help us instead of hurt us?

3. Which impairment of these feelings are you struggling with and what do you need to do to begin to experience the gift of that feeling?

GOING DEEPER . . .

Choose a feeling that you have allowed to take precedence in your life. Take some time and let yourself feel the pain that you have suppressed with that feeling. Now write down how you have allowed this to happen and how you can improve your reaction to that feeling.

FACING THE NEED FOR CHANGE

After surviving a pulmonary embolism, Kristy decided on a lifestyle change. She joined a YMCA in Florida in April 2002 to improve her health, to lose weight, and to keep it off. She weighed over four hundred pounds, but Kristy was determined—and scared. She knew her behavior and lifestyle patterns had to change, so she began by doing low-impact aerobics twice a week and weight training three times a week. As she started to lose the weight, she added more cardiac exercises (such as biking and using the treadmill and elliptical machines). By November 2003, Kristy had lost 205 pounds! Now she visits the YMCA four times a week to maintain her desired weight and to stay healthy.

Change usually takes place out of developmental or environmental forces that urge us to rethink our condition.[1] All of us reach age milestones or face health conditions that cause us to reevaluate our lives. We ask: Are we healthy? Have we reached our spiritual goals? Do we have a sense of well-being? Usually health threats or age milestones usher us to the point of needing to change.

Here's a list of possible developmental and environmental pressures that frequently bring people to the threshold of change:

- Moving from one stage of life to another (i.e., adolescence to adulthood, for example)
- Aging
- Illness
- Life-debilitating addiction
- Retirement
- Inner emotional turmoil

- Marriage
- Childbirth
- Job dissatisfaction
- A promotion or termination
- Death of a loved one
- Divorce
- Health problems
- Societal pressure[2]

SPIRIT

Keep your life so constantly in touch with God that His surprising power can break through at any point. Live in a constant state of expectancy and leave room for God to come as He decides.

—OSWALD CHAMBERS, *MY UTMOST FOR HIS HIGHEST*

Some items on this list are the natural result of life, while others are thrust upon us by our own choices. All of them usher in the possibility for change in some capacity. Those who fail to respond properly to environmental and developmental pressures usually repress the need for change. Some alcoholics continue to drink even after a dismal health report. Some smokers are known to smoke even with a tracheotomy. Phil—mentioned in Day 4—knew that his drinking had become more than just social, even though he checked the box marked "social drinker" on the health club application.

What holds most of us back from experiencing change is fear. We fear what others will think if, like Kristy, we walk into the Y weighing over four hundred pounds. Can you imagine the courage that it must have taken for her to face this fear? We've all had the false belief that YMCAs are for healthy people who are there to simply maintain their great health. But this belief holds us back from change. I wish I could convince people to get involved in change before they are faced with a health scare or environmental pressure. But I believe the avoidance of change stems from low self-esteem.

BODY

> Every time I walk into the YMCA, I am motivated because people are swimming, shooting basketball, dancing, lifting weights, and walking. There are people of all ages, races, and walks of life.

Low self-esteem is the silent locust moth that eats away our courage to change. I see this as a certain kind of pessimism. Over all the years that we have worked with people at the YMCA and Restore Ministries, we find that the majority of them struggle, at some level, with low self-esteem. True, they may have life-controlling issues such as addictions, obesity, risky behavior, or even pornography. But the reality is that underneath there's a deep struggle with low self-esteem.

When low self-esteem sets in, we begin to question our worth when we should be questioning our circumstances. Something is fueling our low self-worth. Sometimes we hate our job, but we're too scared to apply for the one that we desire, and then we berate ourselves for playing it safe. We could be in an abusive relationship or have too many failures to list in one lifetime. But we have to work at finding our true self, and this may mean that a change has to occur.

Most people who face change of any kind have to overcome self-resistance. They feel safe, yet dissatisfied. It's an interesting dichotomy. They feel safe in their addictions or other problems because they know what to expect. And the number-one drawback from change is getting people to take the risk of change.

If we can raise the awareness about low self-esteem and concentrate on ways to overcome our self-loathing, then we will have a chance at changing. But many of us put on our happy faces and head off to work, knowing that we are slowly killing the true self that we long to become. The paradox of low self-esteem is that we project a false self to protect our true desires that we feel will be rejected if discovered. In essence, we say, "If you really discover who I am at my core and what I long to be, then you'd reject me." This is why we hide this inner longing until it comes out in unhealthy ways. We use drugs to alter our moods. We try to live vicariously through the lives of our children. We perform through a false self to gain approval. We have to work at shedding our false self and allow God to change us into the person that He created us to be.

Richard Leider writes, "With major change, we often confront, as seldom before, our own insecurities and self-doubts as we let go of the identity of the past and risk shaping our future.... Through purpose, we grow by becoming more honest with ourselves and more aware of our gifts that naturally give us joy."[3]

THE PAIN OF CHANGE

In *The Voyage of the Dawn Treader*, C. S. Lewis introduces a character named Eustace—a disagreeable boy who seems to delight in being a nuisance. He travels to Narnia, a fantasy world, and finds himself in a dragon's cave filled with treasure. Eustace falls asleep on the dragon's hoard "with greedy, dragonist thoughts in his ear" and wakes up to find that he has turned into a dragon.

After spending time as a dragon, Eustace wants to be himself again and no longer desires to be in the dragon skin. However, he is at a loss as to how he can get rid of the dragon shell. Fortunately, Aslan the lion comes to his rescue and leads the scaly Eustace to a large well of clear, bubbling water. Aslan instructs Eustace to bathe in the water. Eustace attempts three times to peel off his scaly skin, but each time he is just as rough and wrinkled as before. He realizes that he must let Aslan take the skin off, but he is afraid that the lion's claws will hurt. However, Eustace's desire to change outweighs the fear of the pain.

Eustace describes the way that Aslan tore off the dragon skin to his cousin Edmund. "The very first tear he made was so deep that I thought it had gone right into my heart. And when he began pulling the skin off, it hurt worse than anything I've ever felt. The only thing that made me able to bear it was just the pleasure of feeling the stuff peel off . . . he peeled the beastly stuff right off—just as I thought I had done it myself the other three times, only they hadn't hurt—and it was lying on the grass: only ever so much thicker, and darker, and more knobbly-looking than the others had been. And there was I as smooth and soft as a peeled switch and smaller than I had been. Then he caught hold of me—I didn't like that much for I was very tender underneath now that I'd no skin on—and threw me into the water. It smarted like anything but only for a moment. After that it became perfectly delicious and as soon as I started swimming and splashing I found that all the pain had gone."[4]

In our attempts to change, pain will occur and it will seem, at times, unbearable. But we have to let God do His work to shed the unwanted layers that we have accumulated by trying to fix and heal ourselves alone. The first tear might be so deep that it goes straight to our heart, as Eustace experienced, but after the pain is gone you will start to see a new person underneath—one who is ready to begin a new journey and leave the old skin behind.

REFLECTIONS

CHANGE USUALLY TAKES PLACE OUT OF DEVELOPMENTAL OR ENVIRONMENTAL FORCES THAT URGE US TO RETHINK OUR CONDITION.

1. How has low self-esteem affected your life?

2. If God were to peel off the "dragon skin" of your false self, what would you want to find?

3. What do you really think about yourself? Name one strength and one weakness.

GOING DEEPER . . .

Read Psalm 139 and reflect on the involvement of God in creating you, and the love He has for your life.

HIDDEN PRISONS:
LIFE-CONTROLLING ISSUES

BREAKING THE
CHAIN OF NEGATIVE THOUGHTS

I have memories invoked by the hum of lawn mowers in the distance, the smell of fresh-cut grass on sidewalks, the sound of a golf club making contact with a golf ball on the greens—all of these remind me of the golf course that loomed before us, as my father taught me how to golf. Those were wonderful times. I've never forgotten those summers or the golf swing that I developed under his tutelage. If you and I went golfing today, you would witness the same golf swing that I developed back then. It's like riding a bike—you never forget.

Memory is a strange thing. Dr. Gerald May says, "Sadly, the brain never completely forgets what it has learned."[1] This is the human condition. It's as if there were a chain that connects every thought that we've ever had. Some links are massive; other links we barely remember and can only recall with much effort. Then there are the corrosive links, those that try to destroy every good thought that we've ever had, like a cancer, multiplying before we even begin to recognize them.

It would be great if our minds could remember only pleasant things, but memory is no respecter of events. Memory interacts with the stimuli in our lives. This is why hearing a song may remind us of certain times in our lives. Memory involves the integration of thoughts, past and present. We also tend to associate negative thoughts of failure with our self-worth.

We can ask ourselves, "Am I more likely to remember positive memories, as well as negative ones?" If we can't balance the two, then we have disintegration. Disintegration happens when we allow negative thoughts to dominate our minds, and this causes us to be imbalanced. Then negative thoughts form one long chain of bad memories.

Psychologist Arthur Freeman writes, "Remember that the more you repeat something, the more likely you are to keep it in the front of your mind. When you continue to review a mistake, a missed opportunity, or a wrong done to you in the past, you keep the memory fresh, the injury current, the loss immediate, and the pain fresh."[2]

SPIRIT

Our Lord's confidence in God, and in what God's grace could do for anyone, was so perfect that He never despaired, never giving up hope for any person.

—OSWALD CHAMBERS, *MY UTMOST FOR HIS HIGHEST*

Negative patterns of thinking that get repeated over and over again in our minds become deeply ingrained, causing us to approach life from learned patterns of helplessness, just as I approach golf today by the golf swings that my father taught me almost forty-five years ago.

Psychologists believe that negative thoughts are a result of rumination, a close cousin to brooding. Martin Seligman writes, "The more you are inclined to ruminate, the more it arises. The more it arises, the more depressed you will be. Brooding, thinking about how bad things are, starts the sequence. Ruminators get this chain going all the time. Any reminder of the original threat causes them to run off the whole pessimism-rumination chain."[3]

This chain of negative thoughts needs to be broken. Once we fall into the trap, it is easy to link several bad occurrences together, such as linking the failure that we experienced in 1986 with the one in 1991, and the one in 1999, followed by the one in 2005. These failures, when linked together, collectively create feelings of despair. We begin to believe that our whole life can be summed up by these events.

The way to break the rumination chain is by putting together a chain of good thoughts. This method is called diversionary tactics, in which you divert one set of thoughts by substituting another. Dr. Freeman says, "Diversionary tactics can be very effective in changing your mood and helping you to forget, because they interrupt the constant repetition of those thoughts that put you in a bad mood in the first place."[4]

Say you need to lose twenty pounds, and instead of thinking that you can't do it, you start a new chain of thoughts by telling yourself, "I can change my weight." Then add another thought: "I'm going to watch what I eat because eating plays a part in my being overweight." Then the next thought could be, "I'm going to join the YMCA or some other health club and begin to work out." All of these thoughts linked together begin to make a new chain. Scripture instructs us to "be changed within by a new way of thinking."[5]

The new way of thinking begins with a new thought. It's as simple and as hard as that. If we desire life without the present extra twenty pounds, then we have to think about what life would be like without the twenty pounds.

This is the same way that Joe Sobeck had to rethink never playing squash again. Sobeck was the best squash player at the Greenwich, Connecticut, YMCA. Some would say that he was too good at it, but who can blame them for not wanting to get demolished by him? Not many of us would play Tiger Woods in a round of golf: playing him week after week would be humiliating. No one wants to lose on a continual basis. This was Joe Sobeck's problem: no one would play squash with him.

Frustrated by his lack of competition in squash, Sobeck tried handball—but it was not to his liking: handball hurt his hand. This got him thinking about how he might be able to utilize the handball court by combining the racquet from squash with the rubber ball from handball. Out of his dilemma, Joe Sobeck created a new sport—racquetball. He used his despondency as a catalyst for change. He had to think beyond not getting to play squash and rethink his entire situation. He did not "ruminate" on the negative, a term that first meant "chewing the cud." Sobeck combined two sports. He was proactive. We see this repeatedly in the history of the YMCA. Someone invents something great by rethinking the old grid.

Become aware of negative rumination. Try not to "chew the cud" of past failures. One negative thought can lead to another, until we assume that even the future is tainted. Then we begin to link negative thoughts into a chain of learned helplessness. We predict the future based upon our negative chain of thoughts. This is when we give up and believe the lie of negative rumination. We feel helpless.

A negative chain of thoughts breaks when we have our first positive thought. The Scriptures say, "Be changed within by a new way of thinking."[6] This means that our minds can overcome negative thoughts by thinking in a new way about our circumstances. Linking positive thoughts together, the way Joe Sobeck linked two sports, will create a diversionary chain that breaks the negative one. Reevaluate every thought you have. Test each thought. Ask: "Is this thought leading to new thoughts or back to bondage?" Every positive thought will lead us further along the journey to freedom.

REFLECTIONS

NEGATIVE PATTERNS OF THINKING THAT GET REPEATED IN OUR MINDS CAN BECOME DEEPLY INGRAINED BELIEFS.

1. What patterns of thinking do you have about your ability to change?

2. How do your thoughts affect your behavior?

3. Write down three constant negative thoughts that occur in your
   mind. Now write down three truths about yourself that will counter
   those negative thoughts.

GOING DEEPER . . .

*Read Romans 12:2 and 5:3–5 to understand the importance of renewing your
mind and the benefit of making it a daily practice.*

OVERCOMING A STATE OF FEAR

Comedian Jerry Seinfeld once said that, when at a funeral, most of us would prefer to be in the casket than the one delivering the eulogy. Surveys show that we fear public speaking more than death.

Numerous organizations today provide services to help conquer the fear of public speaking. One professional company advertises that they can cure the fear of public speaking in twenty-four hours. If that's true, then sign me up! But I'm afraid I won't get my money's worth. No seminar will help me to speak in public like Ronald Reagan.

Fear can take place in many arenas of life, not just with public speaking. Thom Rutledge writes, "Fear is our constant companion, our day-to-day nemesis, and our ultimate challenge. Fear fuels our negative and judgmental thoughts and our need to control things. Fear underlies guilt and shame and anger."[1]

If I was going to tackle my fear of public speaking, I'd join a Toastmasters club. They are the original "fear-busters" of public speaking. In October 1924, in the basement of the YMCA in Santa Ana, California, a group of men assembled by Dr. Ralph C. Smedley formed a club "to afford practice and training in the art of public speaking."[2] The Toastmasters Club has helped men and women to overcome fear of public speaking for over eighty years, which lets us know that fear is vulnerable to our attacks. If we can overcome the fear of change, we have won 75 percent of the battle. Fear is that critical.

The one phrase that Christ used more than any other was "fear not."

He knows that people change only when they feel safe. He knows that fear holds us in bondage and keeps us from enjoying a lifetime of hope, health, and happiness. I know, because fear influences my own life and at times threatens my faith. It keeps me from loving people. It makes me feel hopeless when God promises so much to be hopeful about.

There are four key fears with which we struggle: 1) fear of death, 2) fear of responsibility, 3) fear of isolation, and 4) fear of meaninglessness. Almost all of us wrestle with these fears at one time or another. Out of the four, the fears of isolation and meaninglessness may be the most difficult to bear.

Psychotherapist Dr. Irvin D. Yalom has provided forty years of oversight to group therapy sessions called "process groups." He asked the participants in his groups to engage in a "top-secret" task. They were each instructed to write down one thing that they did not want the group to know about them. The most common secret in the group was a deep conviction of basic inadequacy—a feeling that they were incompetent in everything they did. The next response was a deep sense of interpersonal alienation—that despite appearances, they were incapable of loving another person.[3]

MIND

We cannot escape fear. We can only transform it into a companion that accompanies us on our exciting adventures. . . . Take a risk today—one small or bold stroke that will make you feel great once you have done it.
—SUSAN JEFFERS

We find this to be true in the people with whom we work at Restore Ministries. There is a deep-seated fear of inadequacy across the board. Most of them think that they are not smart enough, good-looking enough, or skilled enough. They say, in essence, "If you really knew me, you would reject me. I'm unlovable." They go through life waiting to be absolutely certain that no one will reject them before they take any kind of risk. They want to be absolutely certain that they will not fail when they change. They want to be absolutely certain that, if they risk anything in life, they will beat the odds. But no one can be absolutely certain of these things, and this is the reason that most people never take risks.[4]

Change is not waiting for us to become perfect. It's like the people who say that they will go to church once they stop sinning. They will never attend if that is their criteria for attendance. Likewise, people will never change if they wait until they are absolutely certain that they will not fail.

There is a central struggle at the core of our being, and that is fear. A fear-based life is one that I am well familiar with. I believe that the most important journey for all of us is the journey from a fear-based life, living in the grips of the debilitating symptoms of chronic fear, to a faith-based life, a life founded in the courage and freedom that only God can offer.

The most universal fear that I have seen people struggling with is the fear that we will be rejected or abandoned if we are truly known by others. If I'm exposed for who I really am, you will reject me, and so we run our whole lives. We run to perfectionism; we run from our potential and hide in false selves. We hide in drugs and alcohol; we hide in pornography; we hide in food, eating disorders, dysfunctional relationships, and a codependency on anything outside ourselves that will take away this fear of being rejected or abandoned.

Fear blocks us from taking risks and prevents us from striving for new things or reaching our full potential. It can become a very controlling, crippling influence. When we stop doing something because we are afraid, we are positioning something to become a phobia, something that we are going to avoid: fear of flying, fear of public speaking, fear of intimacy, and so on. Those who feel safe have a tendency to change more than those who fear.

All through the Bible, God directly speaks to us about fear. Over and over He reminds us, "Be of great courage, do not be afraid!" Even if I'm walking through the valley of the shadow of death, He tells me not to be afraid because He is with me. If fear of inadequacy is the problem, then security is the cure. So, how do we begin to feel secure enough to risk? The psalmist says in the Bible, "I said, 'I am about to fall,' but, LORD, your love kept me safe."[5] Understanding God means that we realize that He is for us and not against us.

It takes a vision and purpose to defeat fear. Much of what I believe can be summed up in a verse from the book of Jeremiah: "'I know what I am planning for you,' says the LORD. 'I have good plans for you, not plans to hurt you. I will give you hope and a good future.'"[6] I vowed that, with God's help, I would no longer live in bondage to fear. And the moment I began to trust God, I overcame fear. What other choice do we have, really? We can worry. We can feel inadequate. We can fear that we will never be loved.

I feared this for years. I was single for an extended period of time in my life. There were moments when I thought that God had no plans left for my life. Then I met someone and recently remarried. What a feeling to know that God had a plan and a person for me all along. Maybe you need to exhale all of the fear and tension that you feel. Now inhale the wondrous promise of God—that His plans for you are good. Draw new courage. We were meant to live in freedom. As the psalmist said, "I asked the LORD for help, and he answered me. He saved me from all that I feared."[7]

REFLECTIONS

FEAR FUELS OUR DESTRUCTIVE RESPONSES TO LIFE AND
STEALS OUR FREEDOM TO EMBRACE OUR POTENTIAL.

1. How has fear influenced your attempts to change?

2. What areas of your life are you afraid to reveal to others and why?

3. How would you live differently if you weren't afraid?

GOING DEEPER . . .

Meditate on Psalm 23. Reflect on what the words in these verses mean to you.

DENIAL AND PROCRASTINATION

Dan woke up one day and decided to change. It was as simple and as hard as that. He stood five feet, eight inches tall, weighed 412 pounds, and had been in denial for a long time. Dan said that, when buying a new car, he didn't compare prices and styles or gas efficiency. Instead, he bought the car that he could fit into. When he frequented restaurants, he asked for a table. Booths were too small, and sitting in chairs with armrests was like being gripped in a vise. He had to ask for seat belt extensions when he traveled on planes, which stressed him out. He hated his life. He says, "When I weighed 412 pounds, I had started making a photo album for my daughters, because I didn't think I'd be around much longer."

Then Dan purchased a popular book on weight management and began to work out at a YMCA in Rhode Island, believing that he needed to do more than diet. This time it was about a lifestyle change.[1] It was about the truth of his condition. It was about getting out of denial.

DENIAL OVER THE LONG HAUL

H. L. Mencken once said, "All men are frauds. The only difference between them is that some admit it. I myself deny it." Denial is the great enabler that keeps us from change. It teaches us to say, "I don't have a problem. I'm okay. I'm in control." It is a self-protective way of not looking at the truth about ourselves. I have seen that many of us are in denial. We believe that no problem exists—like Phil, who kept driving drunk and kept going to jail—but denied his role in his troubles. Most blame bad luck or believe that the police have somehow singled them out. When we start blaming everyone else for our problems, it's a good indicator that we may be deceiving ourselves.

With denial comes blame. Most people in denial want other people to change, and so they blame others. Adam blamed Eve for his part in eating the forbidden fruit in the Garden of Eden. Cain killed his brother, and then whined when God confronted him. Cain said to God, "My punishment is more than I can bear. Today you are driving me from the land, and I will be hidden from your presence; I will be a restless wanderer on the earth, and whoever finds me will kill me" (Genesis 4:13–14 NIV). This may very well be the first pity party in history. Cain killed his brother and then blamed God for the consequences, making God the bad guy.

Not only do we blame others, but we also hide from them. Laura had lived most of her life in isolation before coming to Restore Ministries. Her bedroom was her hideout. Every night and weekend, she huddled there in fear, because the task of maintaining her false self had become overwhelming. In this place of isolation, her addictions thrived, along with her insecurities, even though she thought that she was protecting herself from rejection and pain.

Through her own journey to freedom, she escaped the bondage of shame and isolation and is now living a life filled with hope. At Restore, she found a safe place to be honest and vulnerable, a place to take a risk to overcome her feelings of inadequacy. And this risk needed to take place in front of others who would accept her and point out falsehoods. Dr. Prochaska believes that many people struggle to stay in their isolation because it feels safe there. You can't fail in isolation.[2] It leads to the false belief that you can change later, which leads to the next enabler.

Procrastination is another tremendous enabler. Procrastination is another form of denial. It causes us to overlook our problems. Denial is a rejection of the truth, whereas procrastination accepts the truth but delays the action required to correct the problem, creating a habitual pattern. Most procrastinators live six months in the future. They think, "I'm going to do something about this, but let's just give it six more months to see what happens." We procrastinate because we don't want to confront the truth about ourselves. We don't want to walk down that difficult path; we don't want to do the work; we don't want to endure the pain or the discomfort that usually comes with change.

SPIRIT

> I fear nothing. I am free.
> —NIOS KAZANTZAKIS, GREEK WRITER

Some overweight brides keep postponing their weddings because they can't get motivated to look their best. *Psychology Today* reports that college students who procrastinate have higher levels of drinking, smoking, insomnia, stomach problems, colds, and flu.[3] It all comes back to fear. We fear that what we think about ourselves is true, that we are inadequate to change.

THE PSALMIST'S WAY

To overcome denial and procrastination, we will need to stop looking for a sensational solution or for a perfect program of change, because the longer we procrastinate, the harder it will ultimately be to change.[4] Determination and willpower play a large role, but not the deciding role. God's power, along with our powerlessness over our problems, results in the outcome that the psalmist experienced.

In Psalm 139, the psalmist opens his life to examination: "God, examine me and know my heart; test me and know my nervous thoughts. See if there is any bad thing in me. Lead me on the road to everlasting life" (vv. 23–24). He didn't deny or blame; he simply asked God to change him. It's a huge difference.

If we can get this right, many things will change for us. Notice the psalmist's weakness as he called on God's strength. The psalmist was humble. He said, "God, examine me and know my heart."[5] He knew that, without God, he was powerless to change. He knew that God could pinpoint his problem, so he opened the pain of his life up to God. In essence, he trusted God.

The psalmist recognized his fearful or anxious thoughts. "Test me and know my nervous thoughts."[6] There is another side of denial and procrastination that many people miss. We fail to see how it influences our self-worth. Many of us tell ourselves, "This is all I am. This is all I will ever be. This is all I will ever know. I am a failure." This is often more difficult than seeing the negatives of our behavior. The psalmist admitted his anxious thoughts. He decided that it was time to stop blaming and denying.

The psalmist was willing to change. He said, "Lead me on the road to everlasting life."[7] All that we bring to this journey is our willingness to be led. We need to be willing to open up and allow God and other people to help us change. God may use other people in our lives to help guide us when we pray, "Lord, lead me." This is where community takes on a significant role in the process of change. One of the neat things about Dan's story is the way that he started a new group at his YMCA. With help from the staff at the Y, he put together a weight-loss support group program and opened the doors to anyone interested in joining. He expected a small turnout, but more than 100 attended that night, and over the course of the ten-week program, they lost a total of 916.5 pounds and 644 inches from their waists. The numbers are incredible!

The power of a group cannot be underestimated. Dan says, "I've gotten a lot of people at the end of each group coming to me and saying thank you. I'm not doing this. They're doing this. Everybody is taking care of themselves. Something that started as a very selfish journey has allowed me to give back to everyone else."

If we isolate ourselves, we will procrastinate, remain in denial, and miss the power of an examined life. Plato once said, "The life that is not examined is not worth living." Accountability is important as we begin to think about change. To move out of denial and procrastination, we need the help of God, His Spirit, and other people in a place where we can get the support, encouragement, love, and accountability that we need. We can't do this alone.

Sheryl was one of the most inspiring people whom God brought into my life. She came into my life at a time when I was in despair. We would talk about life and the vision that I wanted to see come to pass. She would always tell me, "I am for you, and I believe in you." She was one of the most incredibly pure, Spirit-filled, loving, godly persons I've ever met. She was like Jesus in the flesh. I told her everything about me; all my depravity was exposed. And she would remind me of God's love. Sheryl showed me grace, the most powerful force in the universe, and it came in the form of a person telling me that she knew where I came from, but she also knew where God could take me if I opened my life to Him. This is probably what those in Dan's group felt—a freedom to change. This same journey to freedom is available to you.

REFLECTIONS

DENIAL IS THE GREAT ENABLER THAT KEEPS US FROM CHANGE.
IT PREVENTS US FROM SEEING THE TRUTH IN OURSELVES.

1. How would you define *denial*?

2. Is there any area of your life that you are unwilling to look at?

3. Name three things that you have put off doing in the past six months. What is holding you back from making change a priority? What insights have you gained so far about why these have not been addressed?

GOING DEEPER . . .

Challenge: ask a trusted friend what areas in your life could benefit from change.

SILENCING THE INNER CRITIC

Warren Bennis wrote about a promising junior executive at IBM who was involved in a risky venture for the company and ended up losing ten million dollars in the gamble. Later, he was called into the office of Tom Watson Sr., the founder and leader of IBM.

The junior executive, overwhelmed with guilt and fear, blurted out: "I guess you've called me in for my resignation. Here it is, I resign." Watson replied, "You must be joking. I just invested ten million dollars educating you; I can't afford your resignation." We can only imagine how the junior executive must have felt to be forgiven. But, like us, he probably struggled with forgiving himself. He had made a ten-million-dollar mistake!

Maybe you've made some mistakes in your career. Maybe you've let your spouse down again. Maybe you've promised more than you could deliver. Now you feel hopeless and foolish, and that small voice inside is cutting you, insulting you, abusing your self-worth. But that voice is a liar. God's investment in us is huge. He created us. He took the time to fashion us in our mothers' wombs. Then He sat at His desk and drew up blueprints for our lives. He knows that there will be mistakes and detours. He knows that humans aren't perfect, so why do we think we have to be?

Inside each of us, there is an inner critic who reminds us of our frailty and faults. Some of the inner criticism stems from something in our past.

As a child, we may have suffered verbal abuse. Some of us believe that we have to be perfect. We believe that we have to be the model parent and the role model for men and women everywhere. We believe that we have to win every contest in the boardroom. We make life hard on ourselves, and listening to our inner critic leads to despair and the loss of self-worth, which often leads to addiction and other risky behavior. We devalue ourselves and place ourselves in the discount bin. This is a clear sign that something is wrong inside of us when nothing we do brings a sense of value, and we tend to believe that our life doesn't matter.

MIND

As we begin to pry ourselves loose from our old self-concepts, we find that our new, emerging self may enjoy all sorts of adventures.
—JULIA CAMERON, *THE ARTIST WAY*

The inner critic stems from a sense of inferiority. We believe that others perceive us as failures because we perceive ourselves as failures. We personify the inner critic, making it the spokesman for the way the world sees us. It nags and deceives. No matter how we perform, it likes to tell us what we "should" have done, not allowing us to enjoy any success. It makes us feel deeply inadequate.

Overcoming the inner critic has been a lifetime struggle for me. No matter what I achieved athletically or professionally, I never thought it was enough. And this led to the performance trap and to my becoming an approval addict. I felt that I must win outside approval in order to feel good inwardly, which eventually split me into two sides—the defeated side and the side that kept up a false front, as if everything were perfect.

When you have negative beliefs about yourself—if you believe at your core that you are inadequate—then you will begin to pretend to be the person that you believe others want you to be. You will develop what we call a "false self " in order to cope with the reality of the issues that you're dealing with versus the person that you want others to believe you are. I've seen this pattern occur with men and their sexual addictions. They use fantasy to escape the inner critic. Somehow it feels safe to them. It's a way to love themselves when they feel that no one else will. Fantasy never makes judgments.

For many of us, abuse was a part of our childhood, whether it was active, passive, emotional, or sexual; whether it was sarcasm, parental overcontrol, or just plain negativity. I met someone in Restore whose mother had left her alone as a small child while she went out for extended periods of time. Her mother would leave behind junk food and videos to console her daughter. As an adult, this young woman struggled with self-worth and an eating disorder. Another person in Restore had a dad who berated him and told him that he was stupid: "You're lazy. You can't do anything right." Over time, he began to believe it. The voice became a hounding inner critic.

When we carry these kinds of negative messages inside of us from our childhood, we will struggle with inferiority. Eventually we begin to believe these negative messages. Then to silence the inner critic, we self-medicate with substances or activities. No one can live with the inner critic without falling into a pattern of risky behavior to silence it.

The inner critic uses comparison to devalue. The inner critic compares us to those who seemingly have the prestige and power that we desire. Never does it compare us to those who have less. It makes us feel as if we are the only ones being deprived of the "good life." This causes us to feel devalued and to feel as if we are second-class citizens.

ALWAYS SECOND-GUESS THE INNER CRITIC

Swimming and aquatics have long been associated with the YMCA, and tens of millions of people across the country have learned to swim at the YMCA. But this hasn't always been the case. In the early years, swimming suffered at the hands of its critics. Most viewed swimming as a distraction from legitimate physical development. Boys in San Francisco, for example, could not use the pool until after they had passed a proficiency test in gymnastics, as if swimming were mere child's play. Of course, those critics were wrong.

MIND

Go confidently in the direction of your dreams! Live the life you've imagined.

—HENRY DAVID THOREAU

We should never devalue someone or something until we understand its positive aspects. Always make conclusions about yourself and others by evaluating not only the negative comments, but also the positive ones. It might work something like this: Say the inner critic points out a negative trait about yourself that makes you cringe. Instead of taking that negative trait and running with it, state something positive back to the inner critic.

If it says, "You are a terrible mother. Look at how your children behave," then you must dispute its claim. Instead of believing the inner critic, focus on the good things that you have done for your children. Being a soccer mom or taking your child and his friends to see a movie the previous week should count as something positive. Be careful not to disqualify the positives. By disputing with the inner critic, you will silence it.

Swimming at the YMCA needed someone to dispute the negative aspects and point out the positive ones. One thing that helped change the attitudes of the YMCA staff toward pools was the development of mass swim lessons in 1907 by George Corsan at the Detroit YMCA. Corsan taught swimming strokes on land, starting with the crawl stroke first as a confidence builder. He developed the ideas of the learn-to-swim campaign and used bronze buttons to reward swimming proficiency.

In 1932, there were more than a million swimmers a year at YMCA pools. In 1984, it was reported that YMCAs collectively were the largest operator of swimming pools in the world. All of this happened because someone became convinced that swimming could overcome its negatives. Corsan refused to disqualify the positive. He understood the value of swimming as an exercise.

Change takes place when we learn not to listen to the inner critic but instead listen to God. It is essential to have people in our lives who can affirm and love us. As we begin to really listen to what our heavenly Father thinks about us, we drown out the voice of the inner critic. This leads to positive change that will heal our souls and recapture our hearts.

Max Lucado has a beautiful children's book titled *You Are Special*. It is a story of a town of wooden characters, called Wemmicks, where performance decides self-worth. Some Wemmicks can jump tall boxes. Some know big words. Others can sing pretty songs. When they do something special, everyone gives them stickers shaped like stars. But those who seemingly have no talents and are chipped and rough along the edges receive gray dot stickers. If they fall or look stupid, everyone gives them dots. Among these dot-littered Wemmicks is Punchinello, who believes that he deserves every dot he receives.

One day, Punchinello meets a very different and kind Wemmick named Lucia, who has no dots or stars. She's just wooden. And when Punchinello asks her how to avoid receiving stickers from the other Wemmicks, she tells him to go visit Eli, the wood carver who made him.

When Eli meets Punchinello, he places Punchinello on his bench, looks over the dots, and says, "Looks like you've been given some bad marks."

"I've tried real hard."

"Oh, you don't have to defend yourself to me, child. I don't care what the other Wemmicks think . . . and you shouldn't, either. . . . You are special!"

Punchinello says, "Me, special? Why? I can't walk fast. I can't jump. My paint is peeling. Why do I matter to you?"

Eli places his hands on Punchinello's shoulders and says, "Because you are mine. That's why you matter to me."

Every day, Punchinello visits with Eli and hears how special he is—and his dots start hitting the ground. Punchinello refuses to believe what the other Wemmicks think about him, and he is free from a life of gray dots.[1]

There is a God who values you because He made you and loves you just as you are, and the more you are open to hearing that fact each day, the more you will realize who you are. You will begin to accept that you are special because God made you, and this will quiet the inner critic every time. As you spend time alone with God, you will learn to know the sound of His voice and accept His opinion of you above all others.

REFLECTIONS

THE INNER CRITIC STEMS FROM A SENSE OF INFERIORITY.

1. What are the negative thoughts about yourself that you struggle with?

2. How do you believe God sees you?

3. What are some ways that you can hear God's affirmations about you so that you can drown out the inner critic?

GOING DEEPER . . .

Meditate on the following verses so that you can learn and understand how God views you: Romans 8:28, 31–32, and Zephaniah 3:17.

ADDICTIVE THINKING

Early pools at the YMCA posed a health threat to the swimmers. In addition to being small, the pools had no filters or circulation systems, so the water in the pools would eventually become filthy. Maintenance would then have to drain and refill them. But this "negative" was solved when Ray L. Rayburn came up with the idea to use filtration systems to keep the water clean. It was a system of replacement. Water flowed into a filter and came out totally clean and different. It revolutionized swimming at the Y, because pools no longer posed a health threat.

Change is a program of replacement. As we begin to practice new self-dialogue and affirmations and visualize the new person we want to become, these new ways begin to replace the old behaviors. Spending time with God and others who agree with what He says about you can function as a great filtration system. This is another picture of being "transformed" by the renewing of our minds.

Time is the maturing process. God needs time. We need time. Over the years, in working with people in recovery at Restore, we have seen every form of addiction. We have seen various life-controlling issues that are deeply entrenched in people's lives. These behaviors, moods, and thought patterns become a way of life. They rule people's lives and steal a lifetime of hope, health, and happiness.

Gerald May defines *addiction* as "any compulsive habitual behavior that limits the freedom of human desire."[1] Anything that puts us in bondage is a sick and sinful pattern, and addictions only contaminate our lives even more. Think of the pools before filtration systems were invented. The trapped water soon became dirty, limiting the freedom of using the pool. People worried about the health problems associated with dirty pools. In addition, it was very difficult and time-consuming to drain the water and clean the pool, so the positives were trapped inside the negatives.

When trapped inside addictive behavior, we become a polluted pool. The dirty water taints everything. We approach life from this contamination. We corrupt our relationships with God and people. We bring them into this sinful pattern, this closed system of contamination.

The more effort we make to gain control, the stronger our addictions become and the weaker our resistance. What starts out as an effort to stay thin becomes an addiction to dieting or purging. What begins as an attempt to set things in order turns into obsessive-compulsive disorder. We use sex as a means to get love, but soon lose sight of the love because we are blinded by the sex. Anything can become an addiction—work, gambling, fitness, overeating, alcohol, caffeine, cleanliness, approval. The more human effort we put into trying to control these urges, the stronger the impulse becomes. When we use addictions as a filtration system in an attempt to cleanse problems from our lives, they only make matters worse.

God says, "Come, let us talk about these things. Though your sins are like scarlet, they can be as white as snow. Though your sins are deep red, they can be white like wool."[2] God offers a different filtration system to cleanse our souls from sick and sinful patterns.

The first element in the new filtration system is an open relationship with God. He says, "Come, let us talk." It's an invitation. Notice that He doesn't say, "Go do thirty-eight things, then come back and let's talk." He says, in essence, "Let's contemplate your life as it is and discuss how I can help cleanse it."

It's true that we never defeat addictions on our own. God is the filtration system that will wash out the impurities. The way to detach our lives from addictions and attach them to this new filtration system is to realize that we can't cleanse ourselves. We are powerless against our addictions—permanently tainted and stained. We need something beyond our own human power. We need God's help.

SPIRIT

> Every blade of grass has its Angel that bends over it and whispers: Grow, grow.
> —THE TALMUD

The second element is decontamination. We become willing to allow God to cleanse us with His grace. We're ready to reach out and take the hand of hope. We understand that we have nowhere else to turn. This is what Jesus alluded to in the Sermon on the Mount: "Blessed are the poor in spirit" (Matt. 5:3 NIV). Blessed are those who understand that the worst poverty on earth can happen in our souls.

One day I was talking to a friend who was going through a tough bout of depression. His life was in turmoil. He was sitting there, talking and gazing around the room, when his eyes stopped. He had fixated on a list of the Beatitudes that I have hanging on my office wall, and he remarked, "I guess 'Blessed are the poor in spirit' means you're blessed when all you have to hope in is God." I think that is one of the greatest definitions of what Jesus meant in that beatitude.

When we come to the end of ourselves and our self-sufficiency has failed, we arrive at a place of total defeat. When all I can do is throw up my hands and say, "I surrender. God, I need You," this is the beginning of real hope and the beginning of God's transformation of my life.

Dr. Gerald May says, "We will never really turn to God in loving openness as long as we are handling things well enough by ourselves.

And it is precisely our most powerful addictions that cause us to defeat ourselves, that bring us to the rock bottom realization that we cannot finally master everything. It's like we see the junk in the pool and ask God for His help. We kept trying to clean it up on our own when the relationship with Him is the only filtration system that works. Thus, although in one sense addiction is the enemy of grace, it can also be a powerful channel for the flow of grace. Addiction can be, and often is, the thing that brings us to our knees."[3]

POWERLESSNESS IS ALL GOD NEEDS

In the movie *Cast Away*, Tom Hanks stars as Chuck Noland, a workaholic FedEx efficiency expert, who knows what it means to control things. He controls his time, his career, his girlfriend, even his thoughts. But all of this changes when his plane crashes in the middle of the Pacific. Noland soon finds himself stranded alone on a remote desert island, unable to control any aspect of his life for five brutal years. After his rescue, he tells his friend about the time that he tried to kill himself while stranded on the island.

"I was never going to get off that island. I was going to die there totally alone. The only choice I had—the only thing I could control— was when, and how, and where that was going to happen.

"So, I made a rope and I went up to the summit to hang myself. I had to test it, of course, so I used a log . . . and the weight of the log snapped the limb of the tree. I couldn't even kill myself the way I wanted to. Then a warm feeling came over me like a blanket when I realized that I had power over nothing."

Almost everyone will eventually reach a moment of clarity when they realize that they can't control every aspect of their lives. Human strength is limited. The true source of change happens when we admit that we're powerless. We put our hope for change in God's power. "If anyone belongs to Christ, there is a new creation. The old things have gone; everything is made new!"[4] Become this new person.

REFLECTIONS

TIME IS A MATURING PROCESS. GOD NEEDS TIME, AND WE NEED
TIME FOR THE PROCESS OF GROWTH TO TAKE PLACE IN OUR LIVES.

1. What does powerlessness mean to you?

2. What in your life are you still trying to control that may actually be
    out of your control?

3. How does admitting that you're powerless to overcome your problems help you change? How can powerlessness be like a "warm blanket"?

GOING DEEPER . . .

Read Matthew 5:1–12 and reflect on how God's value system is different from ours.

JOURNEY TO A LIFE OF PEACE

I f you made a list of the things that you want out of life, what items would you include? In your youth, you probably would have listed some obvious things—beauty, fame, riches, maybe a luxurious car. But as the years go by, you begin to understand more and more that most of these things might not become realities, and even if they do, you realize that these things cannot satisfy.

The older we get, the more we realize that the greatest of all gifts in life is love, with a close second being peace of mind. The craving for inner peace and contentment seems to be universal. We all want a sense of poise, an inner life integrated with cheerfulness, and the ability to live in harmony with other people. We want freedom from disorder—freedom from distraction, freedom from any strife or dissension—a state of tranquility and quiet that implies a strong faith in the midst of struggles. We desire the peace that only Christ can give: "I leave you peace; my peace I give you. I do not give it to you as the world does. So don't let your hearts be troubled or afraid."[1]

Many of us live fear-based lives. One of the attributes of living in fear is that we're always in need, which causes us to live in a state of anxiety. We worry about our children, our jobs, our health, and then we worry about terrorism and all the other things that are out of our control. We can't control everything with absolute assurance. These mysteries of life can wake us at night and cause us to stare at the ceiling in a state of anxiety. They can make our chest hurt. They can put our stomach in knots. But the journey of peace begins when we realize that we can't control everything. When we let go of the uncontrollable, we discover a state of peace that produces an inner life of serenity, a feeling of warmth and contentment that the world can't offer.

The first barrier keeping us from experiencing peace is thinking that we need to control every aspect of our lives. In Day 11, we learned that the true source of change happens when we admit that we're powerless. We have to make peace with our brokenness and our inability to make life a fairy tale. Bad things happen in life to good people. There are many things that we can't control—so we need to learn to let go. Don't take life so seriously. Learn to let go of the uncontrollable.

SPIRIT

The mass of men live lives of quiet desperation.
—HENRY DAVID THOREAU

The second barrier keeping us from peace is living out of a state of need rather than a state of faith. When we live in constant anxiety, we can't contemplate change.

CHANGE + ANXIETY = OVERLOAD

Before we can change, we must be at peace with our limited human strength. We must give up trying to conquer life and learn to contemplate the inner life, where strength comes from God. Taking the focus off my circumstances and putting it on my inward relationship with God is the beginning of peace. It makes room for gratitude. It allows hope and faith to enter the equation. This is what it means to live in a state of faith.

We find this principle in the Lord's Prayer: "Give us this day our daily bread" (Matt. 6:11 NKJV). Faith must be daily. Our needs are met daily. Instead of obsessing over the future, we need to focus on today. When we take the focus away from ourselves, we will experience real peace—the greatest gift of freedom. It's no longer about human relationships that we believe will make us happy or how much money we need in order to be content. It's the realization that choice is at the heart of peace. Freedom is understanding that our happiness is a choice. The one who chooses peace is peaceful. The mind that chooses contentment is content.

The third barrier keeping us from peace is unforgiveness. In recovery, the phrase is often recited: "Do I want to be right, or do I want to be at peace?" There's a lot of truth in this phrase. I know people who are in bondage to unforgiveness. They can't see that most of the time their unforgiveness only hurts them. They are holding on to an old hurt, trying to fix it themselves yet reliving the hurt. And unforgiveness does nothing to the one who hurt you.

FORGIVENESS BRINGS PEACE

Forgiveness will set you free. A good indicator of the condition of a relationship is how you feel at the mention of the other person's name. Do you get tense? Do you feel resentment? It could be unforgiveness coming to the surface. Face those feelings today; don't put them off till tomorrow, because our tomorrows are uncertain. If you are facing death, money and status don't matter, but peace certainly does.

The point that we should contemplate is this: what would be our response if we only had six months to live? I want to come to the end of my life in a peaceful state of tranquility, knowing that I'm at peace with God and with those whom I love. I desire an inner life that is free of resentment and anger—free of obsession—free of anxiety. Peace is what God intended for each of us.

One of the most beloved hymns ever written is "It Is Well with My Soul." The man who wrote it lost four daughters when their ship sank. His wife survived and sent him the now famous telegram, "Saved alone." The hymn was written from his grief. Several weeks later, as the writer passed the spot where his daughters had perished, he was inspired to write these words:

When peace, like a river, attendeth my way,
When sorrows like sea billows roll;
Whatever my lot, Thou has taught me to say,
It is well, it is well, with my soul.[2]

This background allows you to see the words of the hymn with new eyes. You hear the music with different ears. It is hard to understand how a man could write such a hymn when facing such sadness—unless you know the Author of all peace, the One who gives what the Bible calls "the peace of God, which passeth all understanding."[3] This peace means that we don't have to have life all figured out. It leaves the uncontrollable and unanswerable questions to Him, because sometimes "why" is a mystery.

The journey of peace begins when we stop trying to conquer the world with our own strength and begin to build an inner life that lives beyond the circumstances through the peace of God. A life of hope, health, and happiness begins and ends with peace.

REFLECTIONS

MANY OF US LIVE FEAR-BASED LIVES. ONE OF THE ATTRIBUTES OF LIVING IN FEAR IS THAT WE'RE ALWAYS IN NEED, WHICH CREATES A STATE OF ANXIETY.

1. If you made a list of what you think you need in life, what items would you list?

2. What would it look like to live in a "state of faith," trusting God to meet these needs?

3. What hurts are you holding on to that are keeping you from a life of peace?

GOING DEEPER . . .

Read and contemplate Luke 6:27–36 and Matthew 18:21–35. Strive to see the connection between our faith in God and our ability to forgive.

CREATING CHANGE

UNIVERSALITY: WE ARE NOT ALONE

Universality: we're not alone. I learned this phrase from a therapist friend of mine. We were talking about community and what makes a group a powerful tool for healing, and he said that a group provides a sense of universality, which simply means "we're not alone." Others have similar issues as we do. We struggle together. We realize that we're not alone.

In the movie *Warm Springs*, there is a scene where Franklin D. Roosevelt is diagnosed with polio, and the doctor tells his wife and his mother that his life will never be the same. He will have to deal with the life-changing difficulties of paralysis. This diagnosis pushes FDR into a spiral of despair, and he even wants to give up on his life. Then he hears about a place in Georgia with hot springs where people with polio were going for therapy.

His healing begins the moment that he arrives. He understands the power of universality. He finally sees that others are dealing with the same issues that he has. This place becomes a setting of transformation and healing for FDR where he discovers his life again, and experiences the beginning of hope and healing around other people who are struggling with similar trials. Their strength and courage inspire him. Their honesty and tears move him. Their weakness causes him to risk vulnerability.

Seeing others struggle with similar problems draws us out of isolation and into a place of safety. In the company of those similar to us, we can discover healing. One of the greatest truths about growth and healing is that "I can't do it alone." I need others. I need their support. I need their encouragement. I need their love. I need their accountability. Most people will not abandon us or reject us if we become honest and confess our struggles. Most will meet us in our pain and comfort us.

SPIRIT

> The events in our lives happen in a sequence in time but in their significance to ourselves they find their own order . . . the continuous thread of revelation.
> —EUDORA WELTY

Working with people in the process of change over the years, I've witnessed the greatest breakthroughs when people start opening up and become vulnerable. They begin to speak openly about their struggles. It's as if a monstrous burden is lifted off their souls. They no longer feel alone.

When we come out of isolation and begin to listen to others, we hear stories of struggle that we thought belonged to us exclusively. It's so freeing to hear that other people struggle, too. We realize that we aren't alone—and that's universality. We begin to open up and feel hope. We feel a sense of companionship and community with others. We're in this together. We all want the same thing—to change and get better.

One of the greatest examples of the truth of universality is what I've seen over the past ten years working with men who struggle with sexual addictions or pornography. It's a very shameful issue, very secretive. The nature of it is to hide in fantasy. It keeps them isolated and is damaging to their self-esteem and sense of dignity. But when these men take the first step and enter a group with other men who have a similar struggle, many will break down and cry when they realize that they are not alone. They feel shameful and remorseful. But they also sense hope, as Steve did.

Steve lost his job because of a sexual liaison with a married coworker. His wife separated from him and took the children. He had been very involved in his church and in the community, and he felt deep shame. However, he needed genuine help and healing. He knew this, but he was afraid. He didn't know where to turn until someone mentioned Restore, and he joined a small group of men with the same struggles.

With tears in his eyes, he said, "I didn't think I could ever face this. I was so ashamed and sure that no one had fallen to this depth, especially no one in my position. But hearing all of you guys talk about your struggles made me realize that I'm not alone. There is hope for me. I can be in this kind of group. I can heal here."

MIND

Self-esteem is about trusting your ability to make appropriate choices and cope effectively with adversity.

—DR. NATHANIAL BRANDEN

Universality is always better. It creates one of the greatest dynamics in healing—a place of safety and compassion. When I come out of isolation and connect with a community of people who have struggled the same way that I have, who have felt the same things that I have felt, and who want the same things that I want, this is the journey to freedom. This is grace. It's the meaning behind the proverb, "If you hide your sins, you will not succeed. If you confess and reject them, you will receive mercy."[1] Mercy is what we find in universality. We can't make it alone. We need relationships.

Universality is also the beginning of forgiving ourselves. Healing takes place as we extend to ourselves the compassion of forgiveness, which can be difficult. Sometimes we want to keep punishing ourselves.

We beat ourselves up. But this can make us hopeless, bitter, and even more isolated. We need to deal with our problems first by becoming aware of them, and then by moving to a level of self-forgiveness.

Many of us are shame-stricken. Our addictions and low self-worth have caused us to believe that God doesn't love us—couldn't possibly love us—because of the things that we've done. But somehow we believe that He loves everyone else, because there is no one as bad as we are, no one who has disappointed God as much as we have. When we come into a group and hear other people talking about their doubts, about how they feel that God doesn't love them, that is healing. We need to know that we are not the only ones feeling this way.

A bum died in Bellevue Hospital after stumbling into a washbasin in his squalid room in the Bowery. He was trying to shave, but slipped and hit his head. Someone discovered him lying in a heap and bleeding from a deep gash in his throat. Someone called a doctor, who closed the wound on the spot using black sewing thread, while the bum begged for a drink. They dumped him in a paddy wagon, and then dropped him off at Bellevue Hospital where he languished. He did not eat for three days. He died an unknown bum.

A friend sought him out and was directed to the local morgue where the man lay among dozens of other nameless corpses with tags on their toes. The friend identified him, and when he scraped together the man's belongings, he found a ragged, dirty coat with thirty-eight cents in one pocket and a scrap of paper in the other—all his earthly goods. The scrap of paper had five words written on it: "Dear friends and gentle hearts." *Almost like the words of a song,* he thought. But why in the world would a forgotten drunk carry around a line of lyrics?

Maybe the derelict with the body of a bum still had the heart of a genius. For once upon a time, long before his tragic death at age thirty-eight, he wrote songs that blessed the whole world, such as "Camptown Races," "Oh! Susanna!", and "My Kentucky Home." In all, he had written over two hundred songs that have become deeply rooted in American heritage. He was Stephen Foster, about whom no one seemed to care except one lone friend.[2] What if Foster had been in a loving and caring group, and understood the concept of universality? Would things have turned out differently? Maybe he longed for a group where he could say, "Dear friends and gentle hearts." Maybe that was the message on the small piece of paper.

We all need a place of safety where we can discover healing. Don't stop until you find universality. You're not alone.

REFLECTIONS

UNIVERSALITY MEANS "WE'RE NOT ALONE."

1. Why do you think it is so difficult to change on our own?

2. What has kept you from sharing your struggles with others?

3. What could be the benefits of opening up to a small group of people?

GOING DEEPER . . .

Read Hebrews 10:23–25 and James 5:16 to see the important role that others play along our journey.

RELATIONSHIPS ON THE JOURNEY

An old man walked beside his grandson who rode a donkey as they traveled from one city to another. The old man heard some people say, "Would you look at that old man suffering on his feet while that strong boy is capable of walking!"

In the next town, the old man rode the donkey to keep people from thinking badly about his grandson. But then he heard some people saying, "Would you look at that, a healthy man riding a donkey while he makes that poor boy walk!"

This frustrated the man, so he jumped on the donkey behind his grandson. But then they heard some people say, "Would you look at those heavy brutes making that poor donkey suffer!" So they both got off and walked the donkey. But then they heard some people say, "Would you look at that waste—a perfectly good donkey not being used!" So the boy and the old man just ended up carrying the donkey.

No matter what you do in life, someone is going to criticize you. Some people just feel compelled to give their opinion on everything. But advice can go in two directions—it can be constructive or destructive. We need to avoid destructive criticism and gravitate toward the constructive, which may mean that sometimes you need to avoid those who only tear you down.

The majority of our relationships are a choice. We choose certain friends—some bad, some good. The Bible says, "Do not be fooled: 'Bad friends will ruin good habits.'"[1] Psychologists Henry Cloud and John Townsend say, "Taking a stand against hurtful things that people do and against the things that are opposed to the life that God wants you to create is one of the most positive spiritual things that you can do. God's way is to stand up against bad things."[2]

BODY

> Running makes me a child, a child at play . . . find your own self-renewing compulsion, and you will become the person you were meant to be.
>
> —DR. GEORGE SHEEHAN

First, we need to realize that we may need to change some of our current relationships. We may need to change any relationships that lead us back into our destructive habits. We must disassociate from these people—not because we think that we are better than they, but because they may not be good for us. If we've been stuck in a certain lifestyle for years, one of the greatest dilemmas for us may be to consider cutting off those relationships with the ones who've participated with us in our addictions or destructive habits. These relationships are toxic to our healing, and the separation may help them discover freedom, as well.

Dr. George Sheehan wrote that when he left behind a life of drinking, he became a runner and developed a completely new group of friends who were also involved in running. As his lifestyle changed, so did his group of friends.[3] Dr. Henry Cloud and Dr. John Townsend write, "Relationships carry power—power to do good or power to do evil."[4]

We see this in the life of Joseph in the Bible. Joseph was a handsome servant and house manager for one of Pharaoh's officials in Egypt. His striking features attracted the official's wife, who tried to seduce Joseph.

Slight sexual innuendos began in whispers. Every day she hounded him: "Have sexual relations with me." Though perhaps tempted, every time Joseph said, "No." Then one day when all of the servants were out of the house, she made inappropriate advances toward him again. But Joseph was loyal to his conscience and to God, and he ran away. Joseph had the character and the good sense to flee from her.[5] Sometimes we need to do the same. We need to follow our conscience and remain loyal to God. We need to run from toxic people who try to lead us astray.

Second, there are those who will lead us upward toward our new life, toward the changes that we are trying to bring about in our lives. Find new companions who are on a path to a lifetime of hope, health, and happiness. We need to surround ourselves with these people. We need their support. We need their encouragement. We need their accountability.

Cloud and Townsend believe that we need people who can give and receive the following things: support, love, courage, feedback, wisdom, experience, and accountability. How do we give and receive these gifts?

Listening is the greatest gift that we can give and receive. Listening encourages open discussion. Never judge people while you are listening to them. The fact that they are telling you their truth is important, so affirm that in an encouraging, nonjudgmental way. It always helped me when those around me would assure me that I wasn't alone. I didn't need the advice. I just needed their caring friendship. Often, the biggest mistake that we make trying to help others is forcing them toward action before they are ready.[6] Sometimes we have to allow them to come to the realization themselves.

Effective communication is vital. We need to make sure that we are communicating effectively, and not turning away the people that we need in our lives. This can be tricky. It's what the husband faced when he tried communicating with his wife, who was taking a trip around the world. When she got to London, she called home and asked her husband, "How's the dog?" He said, "Aw, the dog's dead." She said, "The dog's dead?"

"Yeah, the dog's dead."

"You heartless brute. You know how much I care about that dog, and you suddenly tell me the dog is dead."

"What should I have said?"

"Well, you could have told me that the dog was up on the roof. Then when I got over to Paris and called, you could have told me that the dog fell off the roof. Then when I got to Rome, you could have told me that the dog wasn't feeling very well. Then when I got to Venice, you could have told me that the dog had died. . . . Well, how's Mother?"

He said, "She's up on the roof."

MIND

Many people feel personally overwhelmed by constant change. How can you develop self-esteem when you are flooded with fear? Overwhelmed is a state of mind. Being overwhelmed and doing nothing is an easier response than the hard work of thinking through the new demands and claims on your consciousness.

—DR. NATHANIAL BRANDEN

Communication sometimes has a way of breaking down between people. The man in this story adjusted the lines of communication, and so must we, not out of manipulation, but to make sure that we're being heard. Sometimes telling someone a story the way Nathan did after King David's sin of adultery can get their attention. (You can read the entire account in 2 Samuel 12:1–10.) Word pictures and stories can communicate powerful truth in an unobtrusive way.

Never make excuses. Until we suffer our own consequences, we won't change. Our shielding and protecting of others and of ourselves never work. Sometimes we need to step out of the way and let God work. He has a plan. Try not to take on God's role. He is capable of getting others and us where we need to be. Become aware of manipulation techniques. Most of us help others because of our own guilt. Manipulators are good at making other people feel guilty and getting you to do what they want. Anytime a manipulator makes you feel guilty about doing or not doing something, take it as a sign to step back a bit. Helping a manipulator because you feel guilty is called enabling. He or she knows how to push your buttons. So, just take away the buttons.

Let go of the results. Sometimes we want to fix the lives of others when they should be fixing their own lives. Leading them to self-discovery is part of change, so leave the results to God. The apostle Paul wrote about change: "I planted the seed, and Apollos watered it. But God is the One who made it grow."[7] We can plant seeds, and we can water, but God is in control of growth. This fact takes the timetable away. It places them and us on God's timetable, which eventually produces patience. We should never try to fix what only God can repair.

Relationships are challenging—and they may be one of the most decisive factors in our process of change. Our recovery, our healing, our future may very well come down to whom we associate with and how we relate to our loved ones. Work hard in establishing good relationships with others and your change will be successful.

BODY

Walking is one of the greatest mood-altering activities of life. A nice brisk thirty-minute walk in the fresh air releases endorphins, which create a feeling of calmness and well-being. To me, it's the best antidepressant on God's market.

REFLECTIONS

WE NEED TO SURROUND OURSELVES WITH POSITIVE
RELATIONSHIPS THAT WILL ENCOURAGE US TO KEEP MOVING
FORWARD TO OUR NEW LIFE OF HOPE, HEALTH, AND HAPPINESS.

1. How do the people whom we associate with have an affect on our capacity to change?

2. What helps us change the most: a program or people? What is the reason for your answer?

3. What is one step can you take this week to nurture a healthy friend-
    ship with someone else who is on the journey to freedom?

GOING DEEPER . . .

*Challenge: put into action the answer that you wrote for question 3. Keep a
journal of your thoughts.*

THE POWER OF SMALL GROUPS

According to a forest folktale, two porcupines in Northern Canada huddled together to get warm. But their quills pricked each other, so they moved apart. Before long they were shivering, so they moved back together. But soon both were getting jabbed again. They needed each other, but they kept needling each other. Living together with others is not easy. But we learn, as the porcupines learned, that we need each other despite the needling, and small groups provide powerful life-transforming experiences.

A few years ago, Restore Ministries planned some small twelve-step groups for inmates at a local prison to help them overcome various problems. I will never forget the chaplain's response to our program. She said that other organizations do short-term work in the prison, one-time presentations where inmates are asked, "Who wants to change?" and the inmates raise their hands. But then the presenters leave and have no more contact with the inmates, and it doesn't take long for the inmates to slip back into their old ways. So the chaplain was thrilled that we were going to aid the other organizations by forming small groups and building ongoing relationships with the inmates. The chaplain understood the powerful dynamics of a small group, which could provide support, encouragement, hope, accountability, love, and nurturing kindness.

MIND

> It is hope that maintains most of mankind.
> —SOPHOCLES (496–406 BC)

At Restore, we provide different groups for different needs, such as a twelve-step Power to Choose group, a Love Is a Choice group for those struggling with codependency and destructive patterns in relationships, and a group for those desiring weight loss and more active lifestyles. But in the end, the structure of the group doesn't transform lives. The relationships formed within the group's structure provide strength for the members to change. Relationships keep us on the journey and encourage us when we become weak.

When we feel accepted in a group—flaws and all—we will come out of isolation and work consistently toward change. I know people who have been in AA, OA, SA, and church Bible studies for years. It becomes a part of their life. It is an intricate, central point, like a foundation of rock. They know that their group will love them and speak truth into their lives. And this is how small-group relationships become so powerful.

Isolation and loneliness are an epidemic in our society. Many people live lives of "quiet desperation," starving for intimate relationships. And this is why Mr. Hatch's story connects with all of us. Mr. Hatch worked the same drab job in a shoelace factory every day for years. Everything was the same—day in, day out. He had no friends. He spoke to no one. He went to bed early. He went to the shoelace factory early every day. Then one day he came home from work and received a package from the mailman: a Valentine's Day box of candy with a card that simply said, "Somebody loves you."

Mr. Hatch's whole life changed because of this gesture of love. He started his day by speaking to the man at the newsstand when he purchased a newspaper. He began to bake brownies for his neighbors. His outlook on life changed because he had found out that somebody loved him. Then a few days later, the mailman returned to say that he had delivered the box to the wrong address. Mr. Hatch was devastated. He handed over the box with the ribbon attached. Then the card. He watched the mailman deliver the box to the correct house, and then closed his door and proceeded back to his old life. He no longer spoke to the newspaper man or his neighbors. He isolated himself again. He withdrew.

Everyone soon noticed that he had changed. They wondered what had happened and what had become of this outgoing, friendly man. Soon the mailman told them of the mistake. The neighbors decided to do something about it. One day Mr. Hatch came home from work and a huge banner hung over his apartment door, proclaiming, "Everybody loves you, Mr. Hatch!" He dabbed a tear with his handkerchief. He smiled again. He talked again. The man whom the neighbors had lost had returned.[1]

BODY

Exercise can reduce the accumulation of body fat that accompanies aging and can slow, if not reverse, the substantial loss of muscle that usually goes hand in hand with the increase in body fat.

We live in a world where it is very difficult to be vulnerable, to be honest, to be who we really are because we fear that we will be rejected. So why bother with love? This was Mr. Hatch's theory until that mistaken package became a large banner. His experience summarizes small groups beautifully. A small group is the one place where we're loved and welcomed. They offer a place to take off our masks and let down our guards. They create a place to share all of our weaknesses and vulnerabilities. Then we are simply accepted. We are cared for. We are loved.

Grace is extended. In small groups, we get to experience intimacy and authenticity. It's a safe place to say, "I stumbled this week. I am alone. I am scared, and I don't know what to do. I am broken and lost."

Knowing love, in the face of all my inadequacies, is life-changing. This is what we find in small groups. The journey to freedom will always lead me to a small group of people who will love me unconditionally. This is our hope. This is what we all long for—this experience of connection that we find in small groups. We need others to stay on the path to hope, health, and happiness, and others need us. God uses our stories to offer hope to others.

REFLECTIONS

SMALL GROUPS PROVIDE A SETTING WHERE I CAN BUILD
INTIMATE, SAFE RELATIONSHIPS THAT ENCOURAGE, SUPPORT,
AND HOLD ME ACCOUNTABLE ON MY JOURNEY OF CHANGE.

1. What do you believe are some key characteristics of a good small group?

2. Name some of your key supporters. What are their characteristics?

3. To whom do you offer that same kind of support? In what way?

GOING DEEPER . . .

Read Romans 12:4–8. Continue to explore the role that others play in your life as well as how you contribute to others. Keep your thoughts in a journal.

ICEBERGS: HITTING OUR PROBLEMS HEAD-ON

Researchers have discovered that most people make efforts to change around their fortieth birthday.[1] It's as if a bell goes off in our minds, and we jump into action. We decide to face our problems head-on. Confront them intentionally. We schedule workout time at the gym because we don't like what we see in the mirror. We get serious about change.

This happened to Melvin. He turned forty and decided that he needed to tackle his problems deliberately. Melvin weighed around six hundred pounds. He had fallen into a serious depression and was on disability. He lost his house and spent over four months in a nursing home due to complications from his obesity—pneumonia, a collapsed lung, failed kidneys. He was growing closer and closer to the same fate as his obese mother, who had a stroke at forty-three. He knew that if he didn't do something soon, he was going to wind up in the same situation, spending the rest of his life in a nursing home alone before an eventual early death. He knew that was not God's will for his life, so he promised God that he would change, that he would begin to take care of his body.

He became inspired by weatherman Al Roker's experience with gastric bypass surgery, and he realized that he wasn't alone in his struggle with weight. He made the decision to have gastric bypass surgery.[2] After the surgery, Melvin changed his eating habits and began to be hopeful again. He started working out at the YMCA—water aerobics, weight lifting, and cardiovascular exercise six days a week. He also joined Restore

Ministries because he realized that he needed emotional and spiritual healing as much as he needed physical healing.

Melvin had to deal with the issues that controlled his life. Through the Restore process, he discovered that his eating was emotional. It was just a symptom of what was going on in his life. Beneath the surface were emotional issues that had led to his problem of obesity.

MIND

Self-esteem is indispensable to mental health; without it our resilience in the face of life's problems was diminished . . . the negatives had more power over us than positives. The world was a frightening place.

—DR. NATHANIAL BRANDEN

Think of the iceberg that sank the *Titanic*. If you look at an iceberg, you only see the small portion of ice that is above the surface of the water—the vast majority of the iceberg is underneath. In an effort to avoid a head-on collision, the *Titanic* turned, sideswiping the iceberg beneath the surface and ripping open the hull. Some believe that if the *Titanic* had hit the iceberg head-on, there would have been tremendous damage, but the ship might not have sunk.

We have to deal with our problems head-on. Every problem has the possibility to sink us if we try to sidestep it rather than hit it head-on. Beneath the surface of our problems usually looms a greater threat. Drinking, overeating, violent anger, sexual addictions, thrill seeking— all of these could be symptoms of something deeper within us. We may wrestle with deep feelings of insecurity and low self-esteem, so we drink to medicate ourselves. It takes away the edge of pain. It makes us feel stronger and more courageous. Then before we know it, we have a drinking problem. Just like the iceberg that sank the *Titanic*, if we don't deal with our underlying, deeply rooted issues, more—and worse— trouble will be ahead for us. Avoiding problems will not do you any good. Tackle them. Expose them. Dealing with deep underlying issues is a necessary step in the process of change.

NEHEMIAH'S ICEBERG

The biblical book of Nehemiah tells the story of the rebuilding of the wall around Jerusalem after enemies had destroyed it. Nehemiah first surveyed the ruins. He walked around the broken-down wall and wept. How could Jerusalem move on? Their protection was gone. Rebuilding the wall would be too big of a task to take on. But Nehemiah faced the task head-on and came up with a plan.

He assembled a team of people and began to build. Almost immediately, interference occurred. Their enemies were back to stop the rebuilding. They attacked the builders' self-worth. They yelled to the workers, "What they are building—if even a fox climbed up on it, he would break down their wall of stones!"[3] I'm sure laughter erupted among the enemies.

Enemies rose up against the project. There were those who tried to stop the rebuilding, but Nehemiah set guards around the wall as the people worked, defeating the enemy's interference.

Nehemiah did not shrink back from the challenge of building the wall. He hit it head-on in four areas: 1) He made the decision to rebuild and he stuck with it. His vision never wavered. 2) Nehemiah assembled a team to help him with the rebuilding. As we begin to consider the damage of our lives, seeing how we might rebuild, we will need people around us who can build a pocket of protection where we feel safe to become authentic. A place where we experience the freedom to discover our true selves, while surrounded by a healing community of people who extend grace and affirmation to us. Most importantly, they can help protect us from the naysayers who try to skew our vision. 3) Nehemiah ignored the naysayers when they tried to oppose him. There are instances where family, friends, and even our own thoughts can try to oppose our changing for good. But do not give up, and remember the fourth aspect of Nehemiah's character: 4) Nehemiah kept his focus on the end result. He knew how incredible the wall would look once it was rebuilt and the benefits that Israel would receive from it. Nehemiah did not even entertain the thought of the wall not being built when he was opposed. His focus was steady and strong.

Low self-esteem and insecurity have plagued me throughout my life. But I never wanted to deal with those issues. I manipulated my way around them. I avoided. I procrastinated. I ran from confrontation. Dealing with my defects and deep feelings of inadequacy was not pleasant. It made me feel broken. I tried to cope by medicating myself, but I soon discovered that the things I ran to had begun to control my life. My methods of avoidance never set me free.

Melvin lost 324 pounds over twenty-one months. He went from being in a wheelchair to a walker, then to a cane, and finally walking on his own. He went off disability and began to work hard. His quality of life has completely changed. He has been transformed. Melvin met his problems head-on and changed his life.

Long ago, mapmakers sketched dragons on maps as a sign to sailors that they would be entering unknown territory at their own risk. Some sailors would not sail into these unknown waters, while others saw the dragons as a sign of opportunity, a possibility to discover new territory.[4] Each of us has mental and emotional maps with dragons designating certain areas of our lives. We are not sure what's there. We are afraid to venture out, afraid to look beneath the surface of the dragon. But dragons need to be slain. Icebergs need to be hit head-on.

New life is waiting. Be willing to take constructive steps toward meeting your challenges head-on. Deal with them—grow through them—and continue your journey toward a lifetime of hope, health, and happiness. This is what God wants for you.

REFLECTIONS

EVERY PROBLEM HAS THE POSSIBILITY TO SINK US
IF WE TRY TO SIDESTEP IT AND NOT HIT IT HEAD-ON.

1. Do you have a problem that you are trying to sideswipe rather than take head-on? If so, what is it?

2. How might your problems or challenges be an opportunity for growth in your life?

3. How can you begin to hit your problems head-on?

GROWING DEEPER . . .

Read more about Nehemiah in chapters 6, 15, and 16 to see the completion of the wall. Talk to God about how you can rebuild the life around you to better glorify Him.

DISCARDING OLD BAGGAGE

Harland was a failure, the embodiment of discouragement and disappointment. He dropped out of school at fourteen and tried odd jobs. He became a farmhand and hated it; tried being a streetcar conductor and hated that. At sixteen, he lied about his age and joined the army—and hated that, also. When his one-year enlistment was up, he headed for Alabama, tried blacksmithing, and failed. Then he became a railroad locomotive fireman with the Southern Railroad. He loved this job and wanted to be a railroad man for life.

At age eighteen, he married. He had it all: a beautiful wife and a great job. Then failure struck again: the railroad fired him. When he arrived home that day, his wife announced that she was pregnant. It seemed to Harland that he could not catch a break. Then one day while he was out job hunting, his young wife gave away all of their possessions and went home to her parents. He felt like a loser and became extremely depressed.

Harland kept losing jobs for various reasons. Then, late in life, he settled into being a "chief cook and bottle washer" at a restaurant in Corbin, Kentucky. He did fine at this job until the new highway bypassed the restaurant and killed the business, and Harland lost what seemed to be his last job. He retired. A lifetime of hope, health, and happiness had evaded him. He had nothing.

Then the postman brought his first Social Security check. That day, something within Harland finally exploded. He did not want the government feeling sorry for him, and he got so angry that he took that $105 check and started a new business. At the age of eighty-six, he finally became a success. The man who had seemed destined for failure overturned his destiny and got a new lease on happiness, because Harland Sanders—"Colonel Sanders"—started a new business with his first Social Security check. That business was Kentucky Fried Chicken.[1]

BODY

The sovereign invigorator of the body is exercise, and of all the exercises walking is the best.
—THOMAS JEFFERSON

You never know what's around the corner. One set of circumstances can set into motion a domino effect of great things in your life. But there will be failures, disappointments, setbacks, taxes, health complications, wayward children, and other problems. Life has its baggage—those things that weigh us down and keep us stuck in a disappointing life.

Once we've decided to enter the process of change, our baggage will have to be discarded. Old habits of overeating and not exercising, thrill seeking, holding grudges, addictions—all of these old habits will have to be discarded. We must let go of these things because any baggage on the journey to freedom will weigh us down, discourage us, and keep us in bondage.

BATTLE IN THE TRENCHES

In 1 Kings 18–19, a battle took place between Elijah and the prophets of Baal at a place called Mount Carmel. It was a real "battle in the trenches."

The situation seemed hopeless: 450 prophets of Baal against Elijah, God's only prophet. But when Elijah cried out to the Lord, God sent fire from heaven and demonstrated His power as the one true God over the false gods that the people were serving.

SPIRIT

One does not discover new lands without consenting to lose sight of the shore for a very long time.

—ANDRÉ GIDE

The people immediately knelt in worship, crying out, "The LORD, He is God." You would think that Elijah was on the road to an early victory, but Queen Jezebel heard that Elijah had killed the prophets of the god that she worshiped, and she put a bounty on his head. She wanted to kill him. And the man who had just defeated the prophets of Baal ran away in shivering fear. He ran for Beersheba, the southern limit of the land, and then walked another full day into the wilderness. He found a shade tree, plopped down, and said, "That's it. Take my life, LORD. I can't live like this any longer." One minute Elijah was on top of the mountain, and soon after he became so discouraged that he wanted to die.[2]

On the journey to freedom we don't get rid of our baggage all at once. New obstacles will present themselves, and old wounds may resurface. They may even make us run for a shade tree where we just want to give up and die. Beginning the process of change with these obstacles and expectations in mind will help us understand that this journey is a progression, not a destination of complete victory in this lifetime.

We can learn at least three things from Elijah's story. First, Elijah forgot that it was God's power that he needed, not his own strength. We do the same thing. God transforms us, and we learn a new way of life. Then we tell God, "Thanks! I can handle it from here." But we can't. Before long, temptation wears us down. Then we revert to an old pattern of living. We relapse, forgetting how God pulled us through. We get overconfident and feel that we can go it alone. But then we quickly realize that we can't.

Second, Elijah focused solely on the problem, not on God's power to deliver Him. If you do relapse into old ways of thinking and behaving, stay focused on moving toward your goal, not on the failure of relapse. Focus on recovering from your setbacks. And that's all it is—a setback. We can always move forward by renewing a relationship with God based on our powerlessness over our problem.

Third, Elijah isolated himself. He ran away. He escaped and collapsed under a tree with thoughts of failure. It's an easy thing to do, and we do it as well. It's easy to hide. But isolation will only make things worse. We need support and encouragement, and we especially need God.

The reality was that Elijah was discouraged. Just like Elijah, we start to look at life through the filter of our own strength. Then we hear the whisper of the inner critic: "I knew this wouldn't work out. I knew this was too good to be true. You are hopeless. You will never be able to stay on track." The inner critic drives us to a deeper sense of self-pity, and this is where our discouragement thrives.

But God pursued Elijah. He didn't turn His back in disgust. Instead, God held him accountable. When I was a little boy, I'd run away, and my parents would come and find me. They'd say, "What are you doing here?" and I'd shrug my shoulders. Then lovingly and gently, they guided me home. They wanted me to be safe because they loved me. To me, that is the whole story of the Bible: a loving Father who pursues His children.

It's a long journey, this journey to freedom. The Bible says about this journey: "We have around us many people whose lives tell us what faith means. So let us run the race that is before us and never give up. We should remove from our lives anything that would get in the way and the sin that so easily holds us back."[3] So, be patient. Keep your focus on God. Ask for support. Take it one day at a time. Think of Colonel Sanders. Think of his failures. Then think of what he did with that $105 check.

REFLECTIONS

ONE SET OF CIRCUMSTANCES CAN SET INTO MOTION
A DOMINO EFFECT OF GREAT THINGS IN YOUR LIFE.

1. Where is God pursuing you to make some changes in your life?

2. When have you experienced a victory that was quickly followed by
    a defeat? Recount that experience below.

3. What principles can you take away from Elijah's story that will help you come back from a defeat?

GOING DEEPER . . .

Read the story about the prodigal son in Luke 15:11–32. See how God can heal us after a defeat.

DO IT NOW: LIVING THE DASH

A group of business professors placed four monkeys in a room with a tall pole in the center. Suspended at the top of the pole was a bunch of bananas. One of the hungry monkeys started climbing the pole to get something to eat, but just as he reached out to grab a banana, the experimenters blasted him with cold water. Squealing, the monkey scampered down the pole and abandoned his attempt to feed himself. Each monkey made a similar attempt and was drenched with cold water. After attempting a few more times, they finally gave up.

The researchers then removed one of the monkeys from the room and replaced him with a new monkey. As the newcomer began to climb the pole to get the bananas, the other three monkeys grabbed him and pulled him down to the ground. It was a brave act of rescue. They'd tried and failed. They'd felt the cold water in their faces. So, after the new monkey tried to climb the pole several times and was dragged down by the others, he, too, gave up and never attempted to climb the pole again.

The researchers continued to replace the original monkeys, one by one, and each time a new monkey attempted to get the bananas, the other monkeys would again drag him down before he could reach the fruit. In time, the room contained only new monkeys who never attempted to climb the pole for bananas, even though they themselves had never received a cold shower.

Our lives can easily mirror this experiment. We give up on our dreams after a few failed attempts. We stop looking up, but we really don't know why. The urgency of life becomes a lull. We sleep. We stop dreaming. We begin to medicate. We accept the norm even though we have a deep longing for more. But it never works, and this is our only journey. We only get one shot at life, and we must live it to the fullest.

SPIRIT

The tragedy of man is what dies inside himself while he still lives.
—ALBERT SCHWEITZER

THE DASH

If you look at a tombstone, you will see the year that the deceased was born and the year that he died. In between those dates is a dash—representing all the years between birth and death. If I died today, my dash would be between the years 1954 and 2008. But I haven't died yet, so my dash is not complete. But it's possible to lose the urgency of the dash. As some say, "In life there are no dress rehearsals." This is our only journey, but we must begin to believe once again that the pole is worth climbing. The itsy-bitsy spider kept climbing the waterspout because it believed that the sun would shine again, no matter how many times the blast of water washed it out. We have to believe again—believe that the dash is worth living.

However, the dash requires effort. It takes energy to climb the pole with three other monkeys pulling at our heels. Most accomplishments come through tremendous perseverance. We all face the noonday demon: the drudgery of our jobs, our drab existence, the meager pay. The Bible says that life is like running a race. There's the start, the middle, the end. The final lap is the hardest. The middle is where we spend the bulk of life—the dash is where we truly live.

None of us knows when the dash will end. There is no better time for change than now. Mark Twain once said, "Never put off until tomorrow what you can do the day after tomorrow." We say, "I will quit drinking tomorrow," "I'm going to lose ten pounds starting tomorrow," "I'm going to start exercising tomorrow," or "I'm going to finally get a job that I enjoy tomorrow." But it seldom happens.

BODY

One of the best things to do when you are revved up is to move your body. Exercise helps deplete the stress hormones that are circulating through your body so that you can calm down faster.

—JULIAN WHITAKER, MD, AND CAROLE COLEMAN, *SHED 10 YEARS IN 10 WEEKS*

We need to maintain our vision. One of the great tragedies of life is to be held back by someone else's dash. In a way, this is what the monkeys were doing. They gave up because someone else's dash went wrong. They believed a lie.

We need to run our own race, like Irwin Jaskulski. Jaskulski was born in 1902 in Ukraine. He was too young to serve in World War I, but the war affected him, anyway. He had little to eat. He weighed only one hundred pounds at age eighteen

"So, I decided something had to be done," he said. He set out to change. He began a lifetime regimen of calisthenics—eight pull-ups, thirty squats, and fifty sit-ups every other day. He rock climbed, swam, kayaked, and ice skated. He hiked the Austrian and Swiss Alps. Later, at the age of ninety-four, he decided to enter a one-hundred-meter dash in the 1997 Aloha State games. It was his first race since his early twenties. He entered the race in his age group, set a record, and won. He said in a jubilant burst, "I came, I saw, I won!" He ran it in 25.73 seconds. But the

World Association of Veteran Athletes refused to accept his record. They would not recognize the time, saying that the officials and timing systems were not certified. But he did not give up; he continued training to improve his time.

Two years later at the age of ninety-six, he tried again. With determination, he crossed the finish line in 24.01 seconds. He had cut more than fourteen seconds from the record set in 1997 by Kazuhiko Tsutsumi. And this time there were certified officials. Jaskulski was invited by both David Letterman and Jay Leno to appear on their shows. He told them, "I run for my pleasure, health, and satisfaction, not publicity." Jaskulski was a man running a great race, and running at his own pace.

Every day people of all ages come to the YMCA to reach the goal of improving their spirits, minds, and bodies. Each time I see a young child or a senior citizen walk through the door, I remember that it's never too early to start, and it's never too late to change. This encourages me, because when we stop growing, we stop living.

Some of us may feel stuck in our lives. We may believe that change is impossible. But nothing is impossible with God. The book of Jeremiah says, "I am the LORD, the God of every person on the earth. Nothing is impossible for me."[1] God has a vision for us, a dream for our lives. He knows the plans that He has for us, plans for a hope and a future.[2] He wants to use our lives for His purposes. Either we will answer His call, or we will sit back and let our spirits die within us while we miss the most incredible gift—the gift of the dash. With God's help, we can overcome anything, and we can move forward and achieve great things with our dash.

Start living your dash today! Now is the right time and this is the right place, because the dash will eventually end.

REFLECTIONS

MOST ACCOMPLISHMENTS COME THROUGH
TREMENDOUS PERSEVERANCE.

1. How are you living your dash?

2. What dreams have you given up on after a few failed attempts?

3. What do you need to do to persevere?

GOING DEEPER . . .

Read Hebrews 12:1–3 for some encouraging words on how to persevere through rough times.

HOPE RESTORED

GETTING FREE FROM A SHAMEFUL LIFE

APeanuts cartoon pictured Charlie Brown and Lucy on a cruise ship. As they stand on the deck, Lucy says, "Life is like this cruise ship, Charlie Brown. Some people take their deck chairs to the front of the ship so they can see where they are going. Other people take their deck chairs to the back of the ship so they can see where they've been. Which one are you, Charlie Brown?" He answers, "I'm the kind of person who can't get my deck chair open."

Some of us are stuck in a life that never seems to work. But instead of trying to fix it, we settle for the bargain bin, defeatedly admitting that we are slightly blemished. We discount our lives. We mark down our value. We're stuck because we say, "I'm not worth fixing. I'll always be worthless."

Before my journey toward freedom, I was stuck. It wasn't until I got into a twelve-step program and took action that I changed. I needed to take a step, to get unstuck. I needed to do something. It became apparent to me that I was mourning the past. I kept trying to reach back and rearrange things. I wanted the past to be different. But what I didn't realize is that the greatest bondage in life is to be stuck in the past. And from this point of hopelessness comes the attitude of shame. I keep letting God down, my family down, my friends down, and myself down. I'm so ashamed.

SPIRIT

It is not the critic that counts: not the man who points out how the strong man stumbles, or where the doer of deeds could have done better. The credit belongs to the man who is actually in the arena, whose face is marred by dust and sweat and blood, who strives valiantly, who errs, and comes short again and again, because there is no effort without error: but who does actually strive to do good deeds.

—THEODORE ROOSEVELT

In the movie *The Edge*, Charles Morse and Robert Green are stranded in the wilderness following a plane crash. They end up grudgingly helping each other survive the elements and a series of bear attacks. In one scene, Morse says, "I read an interesting book that said most people lost in the wilderness die of shame. Yeah. See, they die of shame. What did I do wrong? How could have I gotten myself into this? So, they sit there and die. Because they didn't do the one thing which would have saved their lives. . . ." Relentless self-criticism always keeps us stuck. We don't do the one thing that can get us free—which is to forgive ourselves and think of solutions—and we become lost in the wilderness. We sit and die.

Shame isolates us on our journey. Søren Kierkegaard once said that all despair is fundamentally a despair of being ourselves. This is the reason that so many of us seek change. We are tired of being who we are. We are ashamed of the way that we've acted or the way that our lives have turned out. But the difference between those who die in their shame and those who transcend it is ultimately a matter of action. One takes action and overcomes. The other becomes stuck in the wilderness of despair and gives up.

Duke University basketball coach Mike Krzyzewski tells a story about the year that they won the National Championship. Duke played rival North Carolina and lost by a large margin. The bus ride back to Durham late that night was grueling. When the players got off the bus and started to go back to the dorms, Coach Krzyzewski said, "Where are you going? Let's go practice." Unbelievably, the team's best practice of the year came after that loss—and in the middle of the night.

Coach Krzyzewski said, "People have more of a tendency to listen after a loss, or after they make a mistake. The hardest thing is to have them listen when you're winning. That's why sustained excellence is the most difficult thing to achieve, because you feel like you don't need one another for it."[1]

We will all make mistakes and suffer setbacks. Relapse will happen. Dr. James Prochaska prefers the word *recycle* instead of *relapse.* Dr. Prochaska writes, "Recycling gives us opportunities to learn. Action followed by relapse is far better than no action at all. People who take action and fail in the next month are twice as likely to succeed over the next six months than those who don't take any action at all."[2] This goes back to what we discussed in Day 4 about training versus trying.

BODY

The strong relationship between regular exercise and good health has been established beyond all doubt.

—GEORGE LEONARD AND MICHAEL MURPHY, *THE LIFE WE ARE GIVEN*

As we contemplate the process of change, we need to realize that there is a good possibility that we will recycle.[3] Growth usually involves temporary setbacks. There are challenges along the way. The road is bumpy. It's never just a straight line of being on our path and not looking back. We follow a jagged line. But progress can happen. We can grow through trials and tribulations. Just don't stop. Refuse to fall into self-pity. Keep thinking.

Another way that shame can isolate us in our journey is to force us to stuff our pain instead of working through it. When we fail horribly or when someone hurts us, we want to disconnect from the pain, so we stuff it. We cover it with a scab called a false self—a scab that can be knocked off with ease. It only takes one mistake, one put-down by another, one lost relationship, and the scab peels away. And what is left is a wounded feeling of shame. Psychologist Karen Horney writes, "We cannot suppress or eliminate essential parts of ourselves without becoming estranged from ourselves. . . . The person simply becomes oblivious to what he really feels, likes, rejects, believes—in short, to what he really is. Without knowing it he may live the life of his image."[4]

We think that if people knew the truth about us, they wouldn't like us. So, we pretend that we are someone else, and by doing this, we reject our pain. We stuff it instead of dealing with it. Lewis Smedes says, "Some of us deny the pain we really feel. It just hurts too much to acknowledge it. Sometimes it scares us; people betrayed and brutalized by their parents are often afraid to admit their pain for fear they may hate the people they most dearly want to love."[5] Smedes goes on to say that it's like the betrayed wife who shoves her pain in the dark room of the soul where feelings are not allowed to enter. She says, "I will never let him have the pleasure of seeing me suffer for his little escapade with his secretary." And as long as she refuses to acknowledge her pain, she will never forgive him or feel loved by him. She has closed herself off from healing and intimacy. She has closed herself off from all inner beauty and goodness.

Shame injures our relationships. We cannot experience intimacy if we've closed off our true self. This is why we fall in love with objects. They don't require intimacy. To love houses, cars, jewelry, and other stuff is a false intimacy that never fulfills our loneliness. But we believe that, if we can just get more and more stuff, it will finally be enough. It never is. Objects can never provide the intimacy that we crave so desperately. Relating to the world on this level never makes us feel loved for who we are, but for how we look, how we perform, or by what we own. This defense mechanism helps for a while, but eventually we get tired of the charades. It wears us down.

If you feel lost in the wilderness, or like Charlie Brown who couldn't get his deck chair open, then try to get on the solution side of the problem. Think of ways to overcome. Think of solutions. The answer may be inside you and not always from an outside source. Don't allow your problems to become permanent. Think your way out. Find solutions. Team up with others. Let them help you, because the biggest mistake in the process of change is giving up. We must believe change is possible.

If you relapse, don't let it plunge you into shame. Instead, use the setback by learning from it. This causes our heart to be receptive to listening to God. He is always teaching us better ways, but when we think that we can do it without Him, we fail. So, take some time to reflect on your situation. Listen for God to direct you. This turns the focus away from ourselves. It makes us receptive to change. Try it. With His help, you can overcome!

REFLECTIONS

SELF-CRITICISM ALWAYS KEEPS US STUCK. ONE THING THAT CAN FREE US FROM SELF-CRITICISM IS TO FORGIVE OURSELVES FOR OUR MISTAKES.

1. If people knew the truth about you, would they like you? Why or why not?

2. What makes it so painful when we are rejected by someone?

3. How have you built up a false self to protect yourself from the pain of rejection? What would it take to begin to drop that false identity?

GOING DEEPER . . .

Read these passages to see how God wants you to handle shame: John 8:1–11 and Psalm 34:4–5.

THE PURSUIT OF GOD

Mars Incorporated, the maker of Snickers candy bars, has a humorous commercial that portrays a crotchety and vindictive God seated behind a massive desk on a fluffy cloud in heaven. Stretched out in front of the huge desk is a line of people of all sizes and races. At the front of the line, God is pounding a small man with accusation after accusation about his sinful life. At each accusation, the man winces. In the middle of the line, a young, impatient man steps out and yells, "Does this line ever move?" Suddenly a hole opens in the cloud, the man drops through, and God says, "It's moving now."

In a humorous way, this commercial reveals what most people believe about God. They believe that He is a cantankerous judge, long on fire and brimstone and short on patience. Some believe that heaven is a long line leading to eternal judgment, according to our behavior on earth. It is hard to trust a vindictive God when we hold this type of agenda. No one wants a relationship with an abusive God.

Discovering God can be a confusing subject because our ideas about God can keep us from trusting Him. Theologian Os Guinness writes, "But if our picture of God is wrong, then our whole presupposition of what it is possible for God to be or do is correspondingly altered. . . . Faith is out of focus, God is not seen as he is . . . [and] doubt easily grows. Such doubts are the direct result of a faulty picture of God."[1] A faulty view will keep us from having a relationship with God. It will keep us from becoming who we were meant to be—children of God.

SPIRIT

We are not accustomed to thinking that God's will for us and our own inner dreams can coincide. Instead, we have bought the message of our culture: This world is a veil of tears, and we are meant to be dutiful and die. The truth is: We are to be bountiful and live.

—JULIA CAMERON, *THE ARTIST WAY*

In Day 19, I discussed how stuffing the pain leads to the development of a false self. The key to healing is to try to heal the wound of shame and therefore discover our true selves. We can do this in two ways.

First, we can discover our true self by having a relationship with God. God's power is not a petulant force or some kind of harsh judgment. It's a relationship. And as we get to know Him more, His life bleeds into ours, the way it does when we fall in love with another human being. We take on His mannerisms. We live to please Him. We want to be with Him. We want to be like Him. This is how we take on His power. There's more to it than just believing in a higher power. It's a relationship. We accept His love, and He becomes not just an idea or some magical genie to transport us out of our lousy circumstances. He becomes our ultimate Friend and Traveling Companion along our journey to healing.

Understanding God in this way has been the greatest experience of my life. I realize that He might not change all of my circumstances, but I know that He'll always be with me on my journey. I let Him teach me and guide me. This is intimacy with God, and all of us crave it. But it is impossible to have intimacy without being vulnerable and honest. I can't be honest with you or with myself if I feel like I'm standing before a furious judge. I'll cover my inadequacies by using my false self, even believing that I can somehow trick God.

Christ said, "Then you will know the truth, and the truth will make you free" (John 8:32). And this is what we are trying to get at—the truth that we cannot do this on our own, the truth that we are creatures created for God's friendship. We get to the truth by being honest with God and ourselves. We seek a relationship. Then the true self emerges.

Second, we can discover that we are valued and loved by God—even when we may feel unlovable. When we experience God's love in this way, it frees us to be more loving toward others. This is why Christ said of the prostitute who washed His feet with her tears and dried them with her hair, "I tell you that her many sins are forgiven, so she showed great love. But the person who is forgiven only a little will love only a little."[2]

MIND

When we think of happiness, we should not focus on our needs so much as our possibilities, we are unhappy not because of things we lack but because we have potentialities that have not been realized.
—DR. GEORGE SHEEHAN, *PERSONAL BEST*

God does not love us because we are good, but He will make us good because He loves us. Intimacy with God occurs when we acknowledge all of our imperfections before Him. It's impossible to see the truth about ourselves without the help of God. Only God's Word can get to the center of our souls and heal us. "God's word is alive and working and is sharper than a double-edged sword. It cuts all the way into us, where the soul and the spirit are joined, to the center of our joints and bones. And it judges the thoughts and feelings in our hearts."[3] When God speaks to me through the Bible or through another person, I see the truth about myself, about who I really am, about what I have been doing. But unlike the God in the Snickers commercial, God loves me and forgives me, and He begins to reveal a way out of my isolation and brokenness. He leads me to a life of freedom.

VULNERABILITY

It's impossible to have intimacy without being vulnerable. I can't be honest with God or with someone else if I don't risk vulnerability. I will continue to hide behind the false self—never risking and never knowing intimacy. We can isolate ourselves from God even in church. We can be at a Bible study, but be very distant from God. We can appear religious. We see this in the case of the Pharisees, the religious scholars of Jesus' day. Jesus said of them, "How terrible for you, teachers of the law and Pharisees! You are hypocrites! You are like tombs that are painted white. Outside, those tombs look fine, but inside, they are full of the bones of dead people and all kinds of unclean things."[4] Jesus was hard on the Pharisees. He showed more mercy to a prostitute caught in the act of adultery than He did to them. Authenticity and vulnerability matter to God.

My vulnerability started in recovery when I began to drop my false self. I realized that I could be myself with flaws and all. That was the greatest feeling in my life. Then I was open to change. It made me want to be a better person.

Trusting God is the first step toward vulnerability. When we trust Him, it doesn't mean that we will not fail. It doesn't mean that He is a grandfather in the sky who wants us to know only bliss. Life will still be difficult. We will fail. This is what vulnerability is all about—the freedom to make mistakes and learn. It's like the young new president of a bank who made an appointment with his predecessor to seek advice. He began, "Sir, as you well know, I lack a great deal of qualifications that you already have for this job. You have been very successful as president of this bank, and I wondered if you would be kind enough to share with me some of the insights that you have gained from your years here that have been the keys to your success."

The older man looked at him with a stare and replied: "Young man, two words: *good decisions*." The young man responded, "Thank you very much, sir, but how does one come to know which is the good decision?"

"One word, young man: *experience.*"

"But how does one get experience?"

"Two words, young man: *bad decisions.*"

Vulnerability is nothing more than gaining experience walking with a God who knows that experience is everything. He doesn't expect us to be perfect. He only desires progress, and making progress comes down to trial and error. The one constant in all of it is the love of God. He understands, like the older bank president, and He doesn't expect us to know everything about what a relationship with Him looks like. He knows that good decisions are a result of some bad decisions. God is not looking for a perfect person. He only desires a relationship that is genuine and vulnerable, and out of this type of relationship, intimacy can happen. When intimacy becomes the basis of a relationship with God, where we share everything in a vulnerable way with God, then we can't help but change.

REFLECTIONS

DISCOVERING GOD CAN BE CONFUSING. FAULTY IDEAS ABOUT GOD CAN KEEP US FROM TRUSTING HIM. TO HAVE A REAL AND POWERFUL RELATIONSHIP WITH GOD, WE NEED TO CORRECT THESE FAULTY IDEAS.

1. What faulty beliefs have you held about God? How have these prevented you from having an intimate relationship with Him?

2. Do you feel valued or loved by God? Why or why not?

3. What do you need to do to experience God on a deeper level today?

GOING DEEPER . . .

Find a quiet time and place where you will not be interrupted and talk honestly and openly with God about your answers to questions 1 and 2.

A CASE OF MISTAKEN IDENTITY

A college student needed a small two-hour course to fill his schedule. The only one that fit into his schedule was a course in Wildlife Zoology. He had some reservations about the course because he had heard that it was tough and the teacher was a bit quirky. But it seemed like the only choice, so he signed up.

After one week and one chapter, the professor gave the class a test. He passed out a sheet of paper divided into squares. In each square was a carefully drawn picture of some bird legs. Not bodies, not wings, not colors, not locales—only bird legs. The students had to identify the birds from the pictures of their legs.

It shocked the student. He didn't have a clue as to what the answers were. The student stared at the test and grew angrier and angrier. Finally reaching the boiling point, he stomped up to the front of the classroom, threw the test on the teacher's desk, and exclaimed, "This is the worst test I've ever seen, and this is the dumbest course I've ever taken."

The teacher looked up at him and said, "Young man, you just flunked the test." Then the teacher picked up the student's paper, saw that he hadn't put his name on it, and asked, "By the way, young man, what's your name?"

At this the student pulled up his pants, revealed his legs, and said, "You identify me!"

Identity is at the heart of changing our life. Identifying the future, identifying true friends, identifying our weaknesses, and identifying our true selves are all important factors. Who am I? Most of us define ourselves by the world's standards. But our true identity is stamped on the soul from within. We have to do the work of discovering our true selves—the person that God created us to be.

Jane Fonda calls the false self "disembodiment." She writes, "Because I believed that to be loved I had to be perfect, I moved 'out of myself'—my body—early on and have spent much of my life searching to come home . . . to be embodied. I didn't understand this until I was in my sixties and started writing this book. I have come to believe that my purpose in life may be to show—through my own story—how this 'disembodiment' happens and how, by understanding it, we can change."[1]

When we look to others to give us an identity, there will be those who attempt to control us. When the controllers treat us well, we feel good about ourselves. But the problem is that we are allowing our dependency to be on others instead of being dependent on God. This breeds insecurity and encourages the false self to grow. The Bible says, "Do not change yourselves to be like the people of this world, but be changed within by a new way of thinking. Then you will be able to decide what God wants for you; you will know what is good and pleasing to him and what is perfect."[2]

The turning point for Jane Fonda happened in 1998. She made a twenty-minute documentary about her life as a sixtieth birthday present to herself. As she reflected on her life, she had a realization: "The disease to please was in me from an early age."[3]

Many of us become addicted to people-pleasing. We expend incredible energy always trying to be perfect. But it's like holding a balloon underwater—eventually a problem is going to come up. When we feel like a failure, and we run to something to medicate our feelings of inferiority, we are stuffing our emotions. Emotions have to go somewhere—and whether they channel themselves through an eating disorder, alcoholism, or codependency, they will manifest themselves somehow in our lives. We can't hold it together forever. Jane Fonda's struggle with identity manifested itself through bulimia.

In my own recovery, one of the saddest moments of my life was when I realized how dishonest I was and how much deceit, how much pretense, made up my life. I was afraid of being alone. I wanted to be with someone whom I trusted and who understood me. But when our insecurities cause us to move out of ourselves and "disembody"—as Fonda refers to it—then we become a stranger to ourselves.

When I entered recovery, I had no inner identity. I didn't know who I was. But I knew that I craved companionship with someone who would love me. However, I learned that I couldn't really love another person until I first identified and loved myself. It sounds so selfish, I know. But, really, it isn't—it is self-acceptance. All of us live with our actual selves and our ideal selves. There's a tension between who we are and who we want to become. The civil war in our souls is our effort to reconcile the two. And how we deal with this reconciliation is usually where our problems emerge. If we fail to live up to our ideals, we plunge into a devastating sense of inferiority where insecurities abound: "I'm not lovable. I'm worthless."

BODY

> But the real juice of life is to be found not nearly so much in the products of our efforts as in the process of living itself, in how it feels to be alive.
>
> —GEORGE LEONARD AND MICHAEL MURPHY, *THE LIFE WE ARE GIVEN*

Dr. Harry Emerson Fosdick says that there are three unhealthy ways to deal with a sense of inferiority: 1) the smoke screen method, 2) the sour-grapes method, and 3) the fantasy method.[4] Feelings of inferiority cause us to surround ourselves with smoke screens in an effort to hide who we really are. In order to lead people away from our feelings of inferiority, we trump up our life with false accomplishments. We walk around as if we are an advertisement for narcissism. We brag. We tell lies. We con people—all in an attempt to cover our inferiorities. But don't be deceived. Everyone can usually see right through the smoke screen. And by covering up our inferiority, we isolate ourselves. We drive people away. No one wants to listen to a narcissist.

Others use the sour-grapes method, the way the fox did in Aesop's fable. The fox called everything that he could not reach "sour grapes." Fosdick writes, "Watch what people are cynical about, and one can often discover what they lack, and subconsciously, beneath their touchy condescension, deeply wish they had."[5]

Others deal with their inferiority by using fantasy to escape. Unable to fulfill their idealized image, they retreat to a life of fantasy, where everything they wish comes true without the threat of failure. But the danger of fantasy is that it can become more vivid than reality. This is how people get caught up in Internet porn, excessive gambling, extramarital affairs, and drugs that make us forget about ourselves. We involve ourselves in fantasy because we want to escape reality. In fantasy, everything is selfish and safe. Then it becomes so vivid that we begin to play these fantasies out in reality. Fantasy can apply to anything that can become an excessive daydream.

Self-acceptance allows us to be at peace with who we are. We might as well be at peace because, no matter how hard we try, we can't escape ourselves. If we try, we land in the unhealthy areas that we mentioned previously. Alcibiades, a gifted but unscrupulous Greek, was noted as an unhappy man. Someone asked Socrates why it was that Alcibiades, who had traveled so much and had seen so much of the world, was still an unhappy man. Socrates answered, "Because wherever he goes, he always takes himself."

Another benefit of self-acceptance is the quality of our relationships. Intimacy increases dramatically in relationships when both people are aware and accepting of themselves. As I continue to change from my false self into my authentic self, I'm discovering that I can better enter relationships without trying to overcompensate to make you love me. I've discovered the true meaning of intimacy, and I'm not going to wither away and die if you choose to reject me. I'm going to be okay. Now I enter relationships from a place of abundance. I have something to give away. This is freedom—freedom to be happy even when I take myself with me on the journey.

REFLECTIONS

IDENTITY IS AT THE HEART OF CHANGING OUR LIVES. IDENTIFYING THE FUTURE, IDENTIFYING TRUE FRIENDS, IDENTIFYING OUR WEAKNESSES, AND IDENTIFYING OUR TRUE SELVES ARE ALL IMPORTANT FACTORS.

1. Can we find our identity by winning the approval of others? Why or why not?

2. Of the three unhealthy ways to deal with a sense of inferiority: 1) the smoke screen method, 2) the sour-grapes method, and 3) the fantasy method, which one do you go to first and why? Please give an example.

3. In what ways do you tend to put the opinions of other people before the opinion of God? How can you work to put God's opinion first?

GOING DEEPER . . .

Read Galatians 1:10 and Isaiah 16:7. Reflect on how God looks at you. Take a few minutes to talk to Him about your thoughts.

COURAGE IS OUR GREATNESS

Blues Boy's first seven recordings had flopped, and recording his latest song in the vacant room at the YMCA in Memphis, Tennessee, didn't add much hope. If anything, it called for even more courage. The recording was cheap and simple—no editing available. It was taped in mono with no room for error, meaning that if Blues Boy and his band messed up, the Ampec reel-to-reel had to start over from the beginning. But, despite the pressure, it only took them two takes to record "Three O'Clock Blues." The song went on to become Blues Boy's first national hit, and from the vacant room in the Memphis YMCA, Blues Boy became the man and the legend known as B. B. King. B. B. said, "That changed my life."[1]

None of us knows when something will come along and change our lives. But B. B. King's recording in the vacant room at the Y proves that sometimes the most unlikely thing in the most implausible place can become a success. If B. B. King had given up after the first seven flops, he would have remained unknown to this day. Unfortunately, most of us give up before we reach a breakthrough. In America, we spend an estimated $30 billion per year on unsuccessful attempts to sustain a healthy lifestyle. Why are so many people failing? I believe that it has to do with a lack of courage.

I've come to a fuller understanding of courage. When I was young, my definition of courage embodied movie stars such as Clint Eastwood and John Wayne. These men faced down bullets in ambushes, in taverns, in rain that raked the streets and pelted their gallon-sized cowboy hats. They sat around campfires, drinking and talking, ready to put their hands on their pistols to fight things that made their horses whinny in the night. I would walk across my lawn with a John Wayne stride, imagining that I was on my way to find the joker who'd just killed someone in cold blood. Looking into the eyes of these big-screen cowboys instantly convinced me that courage could overcome evil. Their far-fetched stories, long on courage and short on defeat, converted me as they flickered on the movie screens of my childhood.

BODY

Age is irrelevant. You can build muscle and bone mass at any age. Research shows that big gains in muscle mass can be acquired until age sixty. Moderate amounts until age 100!

As I look back over my life as an adult, I wouldn't consider myself a very courageous person. Many times, I've cowered in fear and retreated from confrontation. I was the classic passive-aggressive person who held deep resentment toward others, and then would suddenly blow up and cause great damage to my relationships. I lacked the courage to stand my ground and speak the truth. Someone once said that courage is like a tea bag; you never know the strength of it until it's put in hot water.

The movie *Men of Honor* is the true account of how Carl Brashear became the first black Navy deep-sea diver. There's a scene in which Brashear's father is preparing a field with a mule and plow. His hands are bloody; his life is tough. It would be Carl's life, too, if he stayed on the farm. But Carl follows his dream of becoming a diver, and when his parents take him to the bus station, his father tells him, "Don't you come back here, and it's gonna get hard, and it will be hard." His father knows that the hardest part will be for Carl to keep a resilient spirit. Great courage resides in a resilient spirit. A resilient spirit is one that keeps stepping up to the challenge, forgetting the past and forging ahead. I believe that God is trying to instill in us a resilient spirit. He wants us to face down our challenges. As Carl's father said, "It's gonna get hard, and it will be hard."

SPIRIT

Truly, it is in the darkness that one finds the light, so when we are in sorrow, then this light is nearest of all to us.
—MEISTER ECKHART

Dietrich Bonhoeffer, the great German theologian hanged by Hitler for his repudiation of the Nazis, wrote in a letter while in prison, "I believe God will give us all the power we need to resist in all time of distress. But he never gives it in advance, lest we should rely upon it ourselves and not him."[2] This is true courage—to wait upon God's power. Spiritual courage is not cowboy courage. None of us are spiritual John Waynes. We only become courageous as we understand the power of God within us.

A WINNIE-THE-POOH KIND OF DAY

Years ago, early in my journey to freedom, self-doubt and insecurities plagued my efforts to change. Everything I wanted to believe seemed false. It was a feeling that somehow God's grace had limitations when it came to my recovery. I was on the verge of relapse. So I went for a walk at nearby Radnor Lake, along the beautiful trails where the lake is nestled inside the city. I always liked to time my hike so I'd be at the peak of a certain ridge at sunset. This particular hike took place in the fall. The leaves were golden, and the sun radiated on the lake. I needed this inspirational atmosphere. I was beginning to wonder if God really cared about my struggles. Then suddenly I turned a bend in the trail, and a doe and two baby fawns met me. The four of us stood and looked at each other for the longest moment. God spoke to my spirit and said, "Do you see the two baby fawns? They're not fearful, because they know their mother will not abandon them. She will die to protect them." It was as if God was saying, "Scott, have courage. I am with you, and I will always be with you." It gave me such a feeling of resilience.

The day after this hike, I received a card in the mail from a friend. On the front was an illustration of Winnie-the-Pooh and Piglet walking down a winding country road. Piglet is reaching up to take Pooh's hand, and in the caption Piglet says, "I just needed to know you were there."

FEAR NO EVIL

Perseverance in spite of everything is the face of courage. What motivated B. B. King to walk into that vacant room and sing with such emotion? He said, "When I sang 'Three O'Clock Blues,' I was thinking of how much I loved Lowell Fulson's version, but how I also wanted to put my own hurting on that beautiful song."[3] This is a beautiful depiction of our relationship with God. It's what Bonhoeffer was saying through his prison bars. All of us need to put "our own hurting" on God.

The apostle Paul said not long before his death, "My life is being given as an offering to God, and the time has come for me to leave this life. I have fought the good fight, I have finished the race, I have kept the faith."[4] This is courage—to give ourselves to God, to fight to the end, to remain faithful, knowing that He walks with us in this valley of the shadow of death. Fear will come and go, but He is with us. He will never leave us or forsake us.

REFLECTIONS

GREAT COURAGE RESIDES IN A RESILIENT SPIRIT, AS WE KEEP STEPPING UP
TO THE CHALLENGE, FORGETTING THE PAST, AND FORGING AHEAD.

1. What areas in your life are you afraid to face?

2. If given the opportunity to face one of those areas with great courage, what would you do differently from what you are doing now?

3. What steps would you take today to move toward this great attempt?

GOING DEEPER . . .

Read Joshua 1:9 and continue to talk to God about the areas of your life that you need courage to face.

THE PROMISE OF HOPE

During World War II, the Nazis set up a camp factory in Hungary where prisoners were made to labor surrounded by barbaric conditions. One day, the prisoners were ordered to move a huge pile of garbage from one end of the camp to another. The next day, they were ordered to move the pile back to its original location. No reason was given; they were just told to do it. So began a pattern: day after day, the prisoners hauled the same mountain of garbage from one end of the camp to the other.

The impact on the prisoners of that mindless, meaningless labor and existence began to come to the surface. One day, an elderly prisoner began sobbing uncontrollably and had to be led away. Then another man began screaming until he was beaten into silence. A third man suddenly broke away and began running toward the electric fence. He was told to stop or he would be electrocuted. He didn't care. He flung himself on the fence and died in a blinding flash.

In the days that followed, dozens of prisoners went insane. Their captors didn't care, for what the prisoners didn't know was that they were part of an experiment in mental health. The Nazis wanted to determine what would happen when people were subjected to meaningless activity. They wanted to see what a life would become without a sense of purpose. They concluded that the result was insanity and suicide. The commandant even remarked that, at the rate prisoners were killing themselves, there would no longer be a need to use the gas chambers.

MIND

> Hope requires strength—sometimes all the strength you can muster. But hope also gives you strength. Hope energizes. Hope moves you forward. When you dare to hope, you can do so much more than you ever thought.
>
> —EMILIE BARNES, *THE PROMISES OF HOPE*

Meaning is decisive to human existence. We all need a purpose. We need to know that our lives matter. This is why God says, "I know what I am planning for you. . . . I have good plans for you, not plans to hurt you. I will give you hope and a good future."[1] Hope is important to our future, and the great thing about hope is that God gives it freely. He has a purpose for our lives.

Hope is an outgrowth of faith, for faith is believing in what we cannot see. We can't touch hope. We can't hear it or feel it. It's like the wind. It's like the atoms and molecules that make up our world. It's like television waves and radio waves. You can't see them, but they are all around you. So, hope grows from faith.

Lewis Smedes says that there are three things going inside us whenever we hope for something: "The first is desire; we want what we hope for. The second is belief; we believe that what we hope for is possible. The third is doubt; we fear that what we hope for may not happen."[2] Let's take a look at each one of these statements.

First, we need to realize that desire means wanting what we hope for. Everyone wants something. We want our bills paid. We want our children to stay off drugs. We want a nice house in the suburbs or a bungalow at the beach. We want a better job. We want to remain beautiful as we age. We want to lose weight. We want to become addiction-free. We want to be a better person. How do we get what we hope for? It's simple. We must first desire change to the point that we begin to prepare to take action to obtain a new lifestyle. If we want to hit a home run in baseball, we must first get into the game. We desire it, and so we join a team.

At this point on the journey to freedom, you hopefully have identified your problem area, so here's a brief self-assessment to help you gauge your progress so far in the process of change. Check the statements below that are true.

1. _____ I've told one other person about my desire to change.
2. _____ I'm committed to doing whatever it takes to change my lifestyle.
3. _____ I now realize the impact my destructive patterns have had on my life.
4. _____ I'm willing to get an accountability partner to help me.
5. _____ I'm willing to take the next step and write an action plan at the end of this six-week study to help me change my lifestyle.

Some of you may have checked the first three, but not the last two. This is honesty. But understand, your desires will only come true when you are able to check all five as true statements. Work your way through at your own pace. But make sure that you don't fall into a perpetual state of wishful thinking, where all you do is discuss your desires. Eventually we have to get up to bat and swing at the ball if we want to hit a home run. If we want a new job, then we have to prepare a résumé and send it out. If we want to meet new people, we have to emerge from our isolation.

Second, we have to believe that what we hope for is possible. If we fall into hopelessness, then the next stage is self-pity or depression. Lewis Smedes writes, "Hope builds on possibilities."[3] So, start with one step of faith. Take baby steps. You don't have to do it all in one week. Make some small goals, and then accomplish those goals. As you accomplish each one, it will give you more hope. This is what Smedes means when he says, "Hope builds on possibilities."

I hit the lowest point in my life when I went through my divorce at about age forty. I looked at everything about myself, and there was not one good thought, so I eventually stopped looking for anything good. I was depressed and full of self-pity. I couldn't imagine how I was going to pick up the pieces and move forward. But the one strand of hope that I had was to believe that something outside of my own strength could change me. This kind of hope produced the most honest prayer that I have ever prayed to God. It began as a small voice crying out for help, and then the potential for change began, even when all my logic told me that my life was ruined. Over time, God proved my logic to be all wrong. He opened new possibilities one day at a time.

MIND

No matter what your situation, it is your task to set priorities and realistically decide what is possible and what is not possible for yourself. Discipline yourself to focus on what must be done, rather than on your self-doubt. Most people who avoid surrendering to panic are able to see what they are capable of.

—DR. NATHANIAL BRANDEN

Third, we have to realize that hope itself has an element of doubt in it. This seems to go against everything that I just said, but it really does not. If it is possible for us to swing at the ball, then there's the possibility that we might strike out. As Lewis Smedes says, "Human hope is always a risk."[4] We must believe and doubt at the same time. There's the possibility that the pitcher may throw four balls over our head. But this doesn't mean that we stop going up to bat. Just because we hope for something, it doesn't mean that it will happen on our timetable.

Some of us stop stepping up to the plate because too many things have happened in the past. We've struck out more times than we've gotten a base hit, so we just give up on the home run. Did you know that

Babe Ruth led the American League in strikeouts for six years of his career? But he knew that to get a home run, he had to swing. Hope is a risk, but we must never stop hoping.

As I am writing this book, both of my parents are suffering through extremely tough times. My dad is eighty-nine years old and battling cancer and heart problems. My mother has the onset of Alzheimer's. All of my children are grown and living in other cities, so I'm struggling with the empty-nest syndrome. It makes me very sad when I embrace these things. I want my parents to remain strong and youthful. I miss my children, and each time I pass their rooms, sadness comes into my heart. It makes me remember the Serenity Prayer: "God grant me the serenity to accept the things I cannot change, the courage to change the things I can, and wisdom to know the difference."

W. Paul Jones says that the root word of courage is *heart*.[5] Courage means acting from a hopeful, trusting heart. Then Jones gives a superb illustration of how often life will try to beat us down. The example comes from Ernest Hemingway's *The Old Man and the Sea*. In the story, Hemingway's main character, an old fisherman, has always wanted to catch a huge fish, and finally one day—when he is all alone—he catches it. His hands are bloody from the rope. His body works against the fish. Finally, after he subdues the fish, he realizes that the fish is larger than his boat. He has no choice but to tow the fish back to land. Suddenly, a shark appears and goes after his catch. The old fisherman watches helplessly as the shark eats his fish. Now all the proof is gone. No one will ever believe that he had landed the biggest fish of his life.

Jones believes that more is at stake than the fish in this story. There's a courageous perseverance despite everything that went wrong. Even though nothing of value is left of the fish, the old man is faithful to the end. This is what I think about when I visit my parents. I remember how hopeful and faithful they have been in their lives, and even though the human condition has brought sickness upon them, there's still a courageous perseverance. It's a hope that this world is not the end of our existence. As Jones believes, more is at stake than the fish. The Bible says, "If our hope in Christ is for this life only, we should be pitied more than anyone else in the world."⁶ This world is not the end. But we've been conditioned our whole lives to believe that the American dream is the "happily ever after." Then we reach an age when we realize that the American dream is more like vapor on a highway. The closer we get to it, the more we understand that there has to be something greater, something more at stake.

Even if a shark consumes our gallant effort in the end, we don't give up. We stay hopeful to the end, no matter what. Hope responds even when the outcome is dismal, because our hope is in God, not in the outcome.

Begin to set some small goals. Each time you achieve one, it will build up your hope. It will provide meaning and purpose. The Bible says, "You will feel safe because there is hope; you will look around and rest in safety."⁷ Hope is all about new beginnings. It's about believing in the plan God has for us. We have a hope and a future.

REFLECTIONS

MEANING IS DECISIVE TO HUMAN EXISTENCE. WE ALL NEED A PURPOSE.
WE NEED TO KNOW THAT OUR LIVES MATTER. THIS IS WHY GOD
SAYS, "I KNOW WHAT I AM PLANNING FOR YOU. . . . I HAVE GOOD
PLANS FOR YOU, NOT PLANS TO HURT YOU. I WILL GIVE YOU
HOPE AND A GOOD FUTURE" (Jer. 29:11).

1. What did the brief self-assessment reveal to you?

2. Looking at your life right now, where do you see God taking you? What do you think His plans are for you? Does that bring you hope?

3. If you could take one baby step toward change today, what would it be?

GOING DEEPER . . .

Read Isaiah 40:28–31. Read about how God can help you walk through anything in this life. Talk with Him about where you need strength to change and where you need hope for the future.

REFORMATION VERSUS TRANSFORMATION

A leading business school did a study that showed that its graduates did well at first, but in ten years, a more streetwise, pragmatic group overtook them. The conclusion, according to the professor who ran the study, was simple: "We taught them how to solve problems, not recognize opportunities."[1]

Recovery is about solving problems, but it's also about new opportunities. Once we've emptied out the old life, a new lifestyle should take its place. We never replace one habit for another. If we stop overeating but begin to smoke, we have only reformed one habit by replacing it with another. This is not freedom; it's called reformation. Dr. Gerald May writes, "Reformation of behavior usually involves substituting one addiction for another, adapting to a new, possibly less destructive normality. Sometimes substitution is intentional, sometimes unconscious. An overeater adapts to jogging and yoga; a smoker adapts to chewing gum or eating; a television addict becomes dependent upon guided meditations."[2]

Transformation is the direct opposite of what Dr. May described as reformation. Transformation makes all things new. It's a break from an addiction without replacing it with a substitute. It's the subject of Christ's parable about an evil spirit being cast out and trying to return to the clean house. Christ said:

"When an evil spirit comes out of a person, it travels through dry places, looking for a place to rest, but it doesn't find it. So the spirit says, 'I will go back to the house I left.' When the spirit comes back, it finds the house still empty, swept clean, and made neat. Then the evil spirit goes out and brings seven other spirits even more evil than it is, and they go in and live there. So the person has even more trouble than before. It is the same way with the evil people who live today."[3]

G. Campbell Morgan wrote about Christ's parable: "Reformation is ultimately of no value alone. It is only preparation for worse desolation. The only possible cure for a person [is] the incoming of the new Lord and Master."[4] We dispose of a destructive habit and replace it with the Spirit of Christ. We build a relationship with Him and allow Him to fill the empty spot by asking Him into this void.

BODY

It is never too late to benefit from becoming active. Independent of my situation in life and my age, my health will benefit from becoming active and my life will be better.

In the movie *The Shawshank Redemption*, Andy Dufresne is serving two consecutive life terms in prison—wrongly accused of killing his wife. Andy's determination to escape prison hides behind a stoic demeanor. Only fellow inmate Red knows what's behind Andy's submissive facade. As the days grind on in a brutal atmosphere, Andy begins to trust Red enough to tell him about his plans to escape. He instructs Red—if Red gets out on parole—to go to a certain tree in a field, and there he will find a box of cash for him to use to meet Andy in Mexico. Red sees it as a pipe dream—a fantasy that will probably never happen. Then, one day, Andy makes good on his word and escapes.

After Red's successful parole, he realizes that life as a free man is difficult. He even thinks about committing a crime so that he'll be sent back to prison. Red doesn't know how to fill the emptiness of not being incarcerated anymore. He needs a new "normal." He has to make the switch from prison life to civilian life. He feels lost about how to do this, so he thinks about going back to what he had. To him, prison life seems better than the emptiness that he feels. He even contemplates suicide. Then Red remembers Andy's words and begins to ask some new questions: What if Andy was telling the truth? What if there really is a place in Mexico beside the Pacific Ocean where I can live? What if Andy is right?

SPIRIT

The call of God is the expression of God's nature, not ours. God providentially weaves the thread of His call through our lives and only we can distinguish them.

—OSWALD CHAMBERS, *MY UTMOST FOR HIS HIGHEST*

And so he decides to find out. Under the tree, inside a box, Red discovers Andy's letter. It reads, "If you've come this far, maybe you are willing to come a little further. . . . Remember, Red, hope is a good thing, maybe the best of things, and no good thing ever dies." This is the whole message of God. He says it to all of us: "If you've come this far, maybe you are willing to come a little further."

In the last scene of the movie, Red rides a bus with his head out of the window, on his way to the blue Pacific Ocean, on his way to a new life. We hear his thoughts as he says, "I find I am so excited I can barely sit still or hold a thought in my head. I think it is the excitement that only a free man can feel, a free man at the start of a long journey whose conclusion is uncertain. I hope I can make it across the border, I hope to see my friend and shake his hand, I hope the Pacific is as blue as it has been in my dreams, I hope."

Red put his thoughts into action. He boarded the bus. He left prison life behind. He was transformed by hope. He didn't go back to the bondage of prison life. He discovered freedom—and so can you. Don't settle for a mere swapping of one addiction for another. Fill the emptiness left by the removal of addiction with the Spirit of Christ. Christ didn't come to earth to improve men, but to remake them: "If anyone belongs to Christ, there is a new creation. The old things have gone; everything is made new!"[5] We can leave our prisons behind.

REFLECTIONS

TRANSFORMATION MAKES ALL THINGS NEW. IT'S A BREAK FROM AN ADDICTION WITHOUT REPLACING IT WITH A SUBSTITUTE.

1. Have you experienced that pull back into that "prison" you once had been in? Describe those feelings.

2. Did you end up replacing one bad habit for another? Describe what that looked like for you.

3. What are ways that you can look past the prison walls of your circumstance to see the hope that God has for you?

GOING DEEPER . . .

Read the Faith Saints Hall of Fame in Hebrews 11 to see how these people stepped out in faith even when it was uncomfortable or they were afraid of failing.

OVERCOME OBSTACLES

THE POWER OF
PHYSICAL CHANGES

Robert Roberts was a burned-out circus performer. The Big Top no longer thrilled him. He was tired of the spectacular stunts, tired of the difficult traveling, tired of all of the same faces, all out for a good time at the show. The thrill was gone in his spirit, mind, and body, and he walked away from it all. But he wanted to stay in shape, so, in 1881, Roberts—while on staff at the Boston YMCA—inaugurated a system of exercise that he termed bodybuilding work. He believed that rigorous repetition of weight lifting could build up the body. But Roberts had no dumbbells, so he used leftover Civil War cannonballs. The workout was a success, but the young men in the YMCA found it boring. They longed for team sports, and soon Naismith invented basketball to help keep them involved.

Today bodybuilding, weight lifting, and other individual exercises have become popular in our culture. But most people have a hard time getting motivated to work out. Our mind will play tricks on us, deceive us, dissuade us, keep us in the recliner. It is amazing the excuses we come up with to avoid exercise. Sometimes we lack motivation. Some of us are intrinsically motivated; others get motivated when it is quitting time at their jobs or when the doctor gives an ultimatum. Others struggle with a low-grade depression that exercise could help alleviate. Then there are those who refuse to work out altogether.

Personally, I've struggled with three bouts of low-grade depression in my lifetime. Once when I was in college, once in my twenties, and once in my late thirties. I don't think I really knew at the time what was happening; I just knew that I was sad and confused. But those dark days of the soul taught me a great lesson. During the bout of depression that occurred in my thirties, I was working at the YMCA, early in my career. I searched endlessly for relief, and what I discovered that did more good than anything was an early-morning run. This always made me feel better.

I had no appetite and learned that not eating fed right into the hands of a deeper depression. Six, seven, eight hours with no food lowers serotonin levels, which actually enhances depression. If I ate well—in moderate amounts—every three to four hours, it helped to steady my mood. In the afternoon, I would either lift weights at the YMCA or swim. Both seemed to give me a sense of strength.

BODY

Muscle growth in people ranging from sixty to ninety-six years old was as great as could be expected in young people doing the same amount of exercise.

—GEORGE LEONARD AND MICHAEL MURPHY, *THE LIFE WE ARE GIVEN*

When I go for an hour-long hike on the trails at Radnor Lake State Park near my home, my mind is free to listen to the sounds of the breeze through the leaves—the birds singing, the feeling of my feet on the earth, the sensation of the wind against my skin. Sometimes as I hike near the end of the day, the sky changes into beautiful reds and shades of purple. As I come to the peak of a hill, I occasionally see a turtle, a chipmunk, or a deer, or I hear the sound of an owl. I'm a young boy again. The changes in nature awaken a sense of change in me. Peace replaces the frantic feelings of being overwhelmed by the responsibilities of work and life. I need this refuge. I need this restoration. My heart is beating; my lungs are breathing in oxygen. Energy is being spent. The machine that is my body is being tuned and strengthened.

Exercise creates relaxation of the mind and body. There is a reconnection with God when we use our physical bodies in the ways that they were meant to be used. There comes a sense that we are part of something bigger. We awaken to the profound sense of wonder of the miracle of life, of our bodies, our minds, our spirits.

As I exercise, I include my spirit by thinking of certain psalms that I've memorized that always strengthen me. As I jog or lift weights, I put a Scripture verse on an index card in front of me and repeat the passage until I have it memorized. And as I'm growing spiritually, there's a change in my mental outlook. Optimism replaces pessimism. I'm changing and being transformed. As I meditate on God's truth, He corrects my faulty thinking. When I feel my muscles responding to my workouts, I know that I am refilling my tank with energy. I think of my body as a gas tank that needs refueling. I'm responding to all three areas—spirit, mind, and body—that need a sense of balance. Real and lasting change comes through these three areas. Everything in the YMCA's mission confirms this. It's a place where we can mend our lives spiritually, mentally, and physically.

When we exercise, our body produces endorphins. Endorphins are neurotransmitters produced in the brain that reduce pain and create feelings of happiness, vitality, and well-being. John Gray reports that research has demonstrated time and time again that regular exercise decreases serotonin-deficiency symptoms of depression and anxiety, as well as dopamine-deficiency symptoms of ADD and ADHD.[1] One study showed that thirty minutes of exercise three times a day is seven times more effective than prescription drugs in treating depression. Prescription drugs may be necessary for some people, but for many others, regular exercise and nutrition are the solution.

In almost twenty years of working with people in the process of change at the YMCA and Restore, I have discovered these things to be true. We are whole beings, composed of a spirit, mind, and body, and so are those around us. The spirit that discovers fulfillment in God is free of anxiety, the mind at peace with Him never needs to worry, the body vigorous with exercise is healthy, and all three together make up a short but full description of a lifetime of hope, health, and happiness.

REFLECTIONS

EXERCISE IS A WONDERFUL WAY TO INCREASE OUR
SENSE OF WELL-BEING AND OUR SELF-ESTEEM, AND
ALSO HELPS TO REDUCE STRESS IN OUR LIVES.

1. What physical activities do you like to do?

2. What is a realistic, balanced physical activity plan that would help you be healthier?

3. Who would be a good accountability partner to help you follow your plan?

GOING DEEPER . . .

Find a Bible verse that you can meditate on as you implement your activity plan this week. Write it on an index card and take it with you when you are exercising to strengthen the spirit and the body.

HIDDEN PRISONS:
BREAKING FREE FROM BONDAGE

William Morgan, a YMCA instructor in Holyoke, Massachusetts, felt that basketball was too strenuous for the businessmen at the Holyoke YMCA. He wanted a sport that provided exercise without forcing people to run. So he blended various elements of other games, strung a badminton net across the gym floor, and brought out the bladder of a soccer ball, creating a game that he named mintonette—probably not the best name given a sport in the history of athletics. It sounds more like an expensive after-dinner mint than the name of a new sport.

You may be surprised at what you actually know about mintonette. Almost every American has played this sport invented by William Morgan. It became a big hit with the businessmen at the Holyoke Y. But then there was that cumbersome name, a name that didn't fit. Morgan had successfully blended various games to invent mintonette, but he tried to name the game by using a variation of the word badminton and it just didn't seem to fit. Then one day it all became clear to him during an exhibition game at the Springfield YMCA Training School, the birthplace of basketball. A spectator approached Morgan and commented that the game centered on volleying and should be called "volleyball." Morgan agreed and changed the name.

Morgan realized that combining old names to create a new one did not fit his sport. The beginning of change happens when we question the life that we have. Is it adequate? Is it complimenting who we are, or is it distracting us from our purpose here on earth? Sometimes reassessing and renaming our situations can revolutionize us.

We see this practice all through the Bible. God changed the names of the patriarchs after a long struggle with their circumstances to describe their new character: "Your name will no longer be Jacob. Your name will now be Israel, because you have wrestled with God and with people, and you have won."[1] The name change is an outward demonstration of an inward change. Jacob overcame his circumstances. He persevered. And what we all hope for at the end of the day is to emerge from our struggles a better person.

SPIRIT

God will bring the vision He has given you to reality in your life if you will wait on His timing.
—OSWALD CHAMBERS, *MY UTMOST FOR HIS HIGHEST*

Real change transforms our character when we shatter old ways of thinking. We realize that we've built our lives upon sand. Now we desire solid rock for a foundation, and the only way to transform is to reinterpret the life that we have.

Emotions and memory can work together to construct a powerful matrix of deception. In the movie *The Matrix*, Morpheus tells Neo that the Matrix is the world that has been pulled over his eyes to blind him from the truth. I believe that this kind of matrix can happen in real life. We allow an old way of thinking to dominate our future events. We interpret what we see by what we feel and know from the past. Certain smells cause us to remember where and when we last experienced a certain dish of food, or the tobacco in our grandfather's pipe, or the cologne of a past lover or friend.

Remember the experiment in school where you had to identify a certain piece of fruit placed in your hand while blindfolded. Using everything but sight, you had to discern the fruit's identity using past experience. Similarly, this is how our minds and emotions interpret present circumstances. We compare them to the past. But the problem is, past experiences can't always interpret future events. To do so is to overgeneralize, which is taking the past and generalizing it to all new events. It's similar to what we discussed on Day 4 about trying it once and concluding that it doesn't work. But overgeneralization moves further away from just trying one remedy. It generalizes failure to include all of life's circumstances—past and present. So, we succumb to the belief that there is no use trying. It's the Popeye syndrome: "I am what I am."

Most of us resist change or want to discover change on our own terms, like the story of the man trapped in his home by floodwater. As the waters reached his front door, he prayed, "God, please rescue me." Ten minutes later, a boat came by, offering to take the man to safety. "No," said the man, "God will save me." The floods rose, and the man, now trapped upstairs, again prayed, "God, please help me." Five minutes later, another boat came, but again the man declined its help. "God will save me," he said, and the boat went away. At last the flood drove the man to the roof, where he prayed, "God, please help me." Almost at once a roaring sound hovered above. The man said, "I don't need a helicopter. God will rescue me." The man drowned. In heaven, he complained to God about not being rescued, and God replied, "I sent two boats and a helicopter!"

Sometimes we hold tight to the wrong life, even when it proves to be detrimental to us. We deceive ourselves by believing that a miracle cure will rescue us. Sometimes we interpret outside help as interfering with this miracle. Morgan could have rejected the spectator's advice to name the game volleyball. He could have said, "I want to name the game. I don't need outside help. The name is what it is, period." By resisting change, he could have prevented volleyball from becoming the popular sport that it is today.

Accepting change happens when we focus on the solution of a

problem more than on our personal comfort. It feels safe not to change. We only need to make sure that our resistance is not due to fatalism, because sometimes fatalism creeps in and is interpreted as our fate.[2] But the way out of fatalistic thinking is to reinterpret our circumstances by realizing that there is hope, there is a new way of life available to us. We always have choices. Always.

Clara was a sixty-three-year-old grandmother whose arthritis prompted her to join the YMCA of Greater Seattle and participate in its programs. She took the first step to reinterpret her life by joining the Y. She says, "Little did I know how it would change my thinking, my habits, and my outlook on health and fitness. My weight started to drop, and after five months, I had shed thirty pounds. My body image totally changed. I'm still a gray-haired, bespectacled granny with a few extra pounds, but I feel energetic, successful at maintaining my weight, able to lose a few pounds if I choose, and confident I can meet any challenge in my life."[3]

Clara challenged her old "matrix" of beliefs that held her in bondage. She broke free. She took control of her weight and destiny by shattering her old ways of thinking, and became confident that she could face any challenge in the future. She even lost thirty pounds in the process.

The beauty of the concept of changing spirit, mind, and body is that, when we promote change in one area, it affects the other two. Clara joined the Y to benefit from physical exercise, but she also reaped a healthier attitude in her mind. We don't have to change everything overnight. Like Clara, we can start with one area, one day at a time. Small steps lead to advancement, no matter what the speed. Believe that you can change, and this attitude, coupled with God's strength, will help you form a better way of life. Fate is not our master—God is, and He says, "Come to me, all of you who are tired and have heavy loads, and I will give you rest."[4]

William Morgan believed that he could invent a less strenuous game than basketball, and he did. Maybe his first name for the game was horrible, but he didn't worry about the name in the beginning. He concentrated on breaking free from the old matrix to invent a new game. And when the game came into focus, the name changed. And so will your life—one baby step at a time. This is the beauty of change. The only thing required is the desire to have a different life from the one you have now. Breaking free from hidden prisons is done by becoming aware of what binds us to the past. Finding hope to overcome the prison is as simple as discarding everything that tells you that you will never change. All things are possible with God.[5] Freedom occurs when we journey to new destinations that can't be defined by the past.

REFLECTIONS

REAL CHANGE TRANSFORMS OUR CHARACTER
WHEN WE SHATTER OLD WAYS OF THINKING.

1. How is the way that you are *thinking* about your problem keeping you stuck?

2. How would focusing on the solution rather than the problem make a difference?

3. What is one positive step that you can take today to change your life for the better?

GOING DEEPER . . .

Contemplate the power of positive thinking in Philippians 4:6–9.

LIVING BY VISION

Dick Fosbury was the first high jump competitor to use the flop, starting in the 1960s. He went over head first with his back to the bar. Some people laughed, while others told him that he'd never be able to perfect the move. The straddle method was the standard technique used in the high jump at that time, in which participants vaulted over the bar while facing it, with one arm and one leg leading. But Fosbury dared to modify the standard.

Fosbury said, "I was told over and over again that I would never be successful, that I was not going to be competitive and the technique was simply not going to work. All I could do was shrug and say, 'We'll just have to see.'"[1] But Fosbury proved his skeptics wrong when he won the gold medal at the Mexico City Olympics in 1968. Today, his technique has become the standard in the high jump. It's known as the "Fosbury Flop."

Fosbury trained by vision. Vision asks new questions: "What if I jumped backward? How can I invent a new standard?" This is a different focus from living out of a state of need. In a needy state we ask desperate questions: "Will I make the jump? Will I qualify for the event?" Our inferiority complex overwhelms our ability to excel. We are in survival mode, and some of us just give up after a few attempts. We surrender instead of tackling the situation courageously to discover a better way to jump higher. We accept the limits without trying to push them to a new level.

Part of change is challenging ourselves to a new standard of living. Life doesn't have to be just average, especially as we are starting to learn more about God's heart and vision for us. This is living by vision.

SPIRIT

There is only one relationship that really matters, and that is your personal relationship to your personal Redeemer and Lord. If you maintain that at all cost, letting everything else go, God will fulfill His purpose for your life. One individual life may be of priceless value to God's purposes, and yours may be that life.

—OSWALD CHAMBERS, *MY UTMOST FOR HIS HIGHEST*

When we become preoccupied with our inferiorities, we inevitably get stuck. We focus on the shame of our mistake instead of learning from the failure and getting on with our lives. We think, "I should have been a better person." And the way that we accomplish our need to be better is by beating ourselves up, trying to use shame as a motivator for change.

Others live, not by addictions or relationships with people or things, but with a need to rearrange the past. We often become preoccupied with our failures and never get on with our lives. We live by the need to go back into the past to ruminate about those failures, not really learning from them. We want to undo our mistakes, but this kind of thinking jeopardizes our future and keeps us in bondage.

Drowning in shame and trying to rearrange the past is not the way to move forward in life. It would be like a batter in baseball walking up to the plate and announcing to everyone that he now knows why he struck out the last time at bat. So, if they wouldn't mind, he'd like to go back and replay the third inning where he'd had a 3-2 count, so he can fix his mistake. This sounds crazy, but we do the same thing all the time.

We go back in our minds and rehash old failures. We ruminate. We cas-tigate ourselves. We see the solution that we should have chosen and rake ourselves over the coals for not seeing it when it happened, whether it be ten years ago or two weeks ago.

Life, much like baseball, doesn't work that way. A new inning is just that—a new inning, a new opportunity to hit a home run. When we live from an "I need to be better" standpoint, the moment our circum-stances go wrong, we will plunge back to the depths of feeling eternally broken. We tell ourselves that we really haven't changed. But what if, like Fosbury, we think of a new and different way to jump over our problems, a new way to motivate change?

When we live by vision, we are not stuck in the past. We learn from our mistakes and move on. Our focus is on what we are going to become, instead of what we have been. This is why the apostle Paul said in the Bible, "I know that I have not yet reached that goal, but there is one thing I always do. Forgetting the past and straining toward what is ahead, I keep trying to reach the goal and get the prize for which God called me through Christ to the life above."[2]

Remember in Day 1 we read how Michelangelo chipped away at a block of stone to release the imprisoned angel? Michelangelo under-stood how to live a life driven by vision. He first had to envision the angel, and then with his focus on his vision, he worked to set the angel free. The apostle Paul did the same thing. He had to forget the past because there was nothing there to set him free. His goal was to chip away the past so that he could reach the new goal in the life above. This is why he also said, "If anyone belongs to Christ, there is a new creation. The old things have gone; everything is made new!"[3]

No longer can we use the old as a reference point for the future. It is gone! How can my old life tell my new life what it should be? Thinking about changing, we often say, "I'm not going to be like that anymore," but that is faulty thinking. When we make that statement, we're not defining what we should become. We're only saying that we shouldn't be "like that."

Recovery is a matter of replacement. We replace the old life with a new one. This doesn't mean that all our cravings magically go away. They won't: we will be tempted. We are not trying to put all of our energy into resisting, but into becoming someone different by replacing our addictions and longings with healthy patterns of living.

Recovery is learning new ways to live. To set our spirits free, we need to chip away everything that's not associated with the fruit of the Spirit, which is "love, joy, peace, patience, kindness, goodness, faithfulness, gentleness, self-control."[4] We allow the Spirit's fruit to take shape in our lives, and this replaces our unwanted behavior. One way to accomplish this transformation is to start with kindness, beginning to approach everything in life with kindness in mind. Then add another fruit of the Spirit, such as self-control. Focus on self-control until it becomes your new response to life. The fruit will just grow in your life as you stay on your journey to freedom with others.

Wherever there is great vision, there is great passion. The word *passion* comes from the Latin word meaning "suffering." This means that we will suffer as we chip away the old life for the new. It will hurt us emotionally. But it also means that, if we are temporarily lonely or hurting, we can suffer through it for a while because we know that we are going somewhere. We have a goal instead of being lonely and in pain without hope. Where there is hope, there is the vision needed to suffer through our current circumstances, to carve something hopeful and new out of our failure. Without vision, we suffer needlessly.

When I start living my life out of my vision, the vision ignites my purpose for living and drives my recovery. Now I experience the power of the Spirit moving me along toward the future that God desires for me.

One of my favorite verses in Proverbs reads, "Where there is no vision, the people perish."[5] Living by vision is to set our eyes on what we want to become, and then we chip away everything that doesn't get us to our goal. Soon we will catch a glimpse of all that we can become, and the fulfillment of that replaces the emptiness and longing that we've been trying to fill with addictions and unhealthy relationships.

REFLECTIONS

THE KEY TO CHANGING AND GROWING IS TO BEGIN TO LIVE OUT OF VISION.
VISION IGNITES MY PASSION FOR LIVING AND DRIVES MY RECOVERY.

1. What is your definition of the word *vision*? Do you have a vision for
    your life?

2. What in your life would need to be chipped away for the angel to
    emerge?

3. If you could forget your past and nothing was holding you back, what would your life look like? (Think about such areas like family, career, spirituality, etc.) Use this space to write your thoughts.

GOING DEEPER . . .

Read Galatians 5:22–23. Pick a fruit to incorporate into your life this week. Find other verses related to this fruit.

PROGRESS, NOT PERFECTION

Jack began in the summer of 1995. He was tired of being pudgy around the middle and suffering some painful gastrointestinal problems, so he decided that he needed to change. He wanted to lose some weight, but he never anticipated the change that he would encounter. Overweight and not engaged in any physical exercise whatsoever, he began a strict low-fat diet and lost thirty-five pounds. Then, on a whim, he decided to begin shaping his body. At the time, his goals were modest. He just wanted to look in shape. Having lifted weights off and on since his teens, he decided to return to the YMCA. He'd maintained a membership for many years, but rarely used it. The surprising thing about his process of change was that he enjoyed bodybuilding once he returned to the Y. He admits that his initial lifts were pathetic, but they quickly increased to a level consistent with what they had been in the past.

Jack's decision to begin bodybuilding at the age of thirty-nine left him with what he calls a "considerable handicap." But despite his pudginess and age, he emerged from his recliner and his fast-food diet to discover the right combination of training, nutrition, and dedication, and it yielded impressive results. His body is now lean and fit.

Making progress in our plan of action will require that we show up, do our part, and trust God with the results. If we focus on progress and not perfection, it gives us the determination to stay the course. Most of the time, what we can expect in recovery is two steps forward and one step back. We are a work in progress, not yet perfect.

SPIRIT

> Perseverance is failing nineteen times and succeeding the twentieth.
> —JULIE ANDREWS

There's a saying that high expectations lead to low serenity, and low expectations lead to high serenity. Apart from God, we can try to reform our behavior and try to white-knuckle our way through change, but when we do that, our focus is totally on our performance, not on progress.

Progress is a path of small transformations that take place each day. It's a path of brutal difficulty and sweet success. Plenty of mistakes litter the road of progress. Think about road construction. What a mess! All of those orange barrels, the congested traffic, the steamy blacktop, and the dump trucks hauling rock deep into the night. Road construction is not a pretty sight, but when it is finished, the traveling is smooth. Our vehicles glide over the pavement. But during the process, we get sick of seeing those men in orange vests. We want them to go away quickly, but they seem to hang around forever.

Recovery is much like construction on a highway. The progress is slow, and the rubble of barrels and loose rock is staggering. If we're not careful, we can take our eyes off the goal, become overwhelmed with the rubble around us, and quit.

This is what happened to the workers on the wall around Jerusalem. On Day 16, we discussed Nehemiah's rebuilding the wall around Jerusalem after their enemies had destroyed it. His first task was to survey the ruins, and he walked and wept around the broken-down wall. Then he assembled a team of people and began to build. Almost immediately, enemies rose up against the project. They attacked the builders' self-worth. They yelled to the workers, "What are these weak Jews doing? . . . If a fox climbed up on the stone wall they are building, it would break it down."[1] So Nehemiah set guards around the wall as the people worked, attempting to silence the enemies' interference. They had dealt with the enemies without, but they still had to overcome the enemy within their hearts. When they reached the halfway point,[2] they looked around and said, "The workers are getting tired. There is so much trash we cannot rebuild the wall."[3] They were close to giving up.

Author Rick Warren says about this verse: "Some of you are discouraged because you are under tremendous pressure; your work load is unbelievable. God's message to you is reorganize. Reorganize your time; reorganize your schedule; refocus on your goal. Clear out the clutter and rubble and trivia, the things that are wasting your time. Then reorganize so that you work toward your main goal."[4]

MIND

It is then the truest valor to dare to live.

—SIR THOMAS BROWNE

THE BABY STEPS OF TRUE CHANGE

Our process of change will be marked by new beginnings. We will fail; we will get tired; our strength will give out. Then we will start again, and we'll get better. This is how we transform. Change doesn't happen with one large step, but with multiple baby steps. It takes time. It's like hitting a golf ball. If I've always hit at a golf ball with some very bad habits in my swing, then it's going to take time for the new habits to replace the old ones. Some old habits have been in our lives for a long time, perhaps even our whole life, so we have to keep a realistic expectation of what it will take to change those habits. God doesn't expect perfection. What He expects is humility. He wants us to work with Him and work with the people whom He has put in our life to help make progress a reality.

Dr. Gerald May says that our addictions divide our will, splitting it right down the middle.[5] A part of us sincerely wants to change, but there's another part, just as strong, that wants to hold on to our addictions or destructive patterns. This is why it is crucial to surround ourselves with accountability partners and a small group. This is where sane voices instruct and encourage us to get back on our feet. Determination and perseverance are wonderful. We need courage in order to succeed. But mostly, we need to be aware of our progress over time. It will happen if we just keep showing up and working on it.

INTRINSIC VERSUS EXTRINSIC MOTIVATION

Some of us get extrinsically motivated to change. We think, "I'm going to lose my driver's license if I don't stop drinking;" or, "My wife is going to leave me if I don't stop looking at pornography." Extrinsic negative consequences will motivate us, but they fail to sustain change over the long haul, because when we get back those things that we've lost (such as a driver's license), we will lose the extrinsic motivation, and the tendency to fall back into the old lifestyle becomes natural. Motivation has to be sustained, and we do this by being intrinsically motivated.

When someone is intrinsically motivated, it's not about making anyone happy or trying to avoid a consequence. It's an internal desire to work together with God from a perspective of "I want to be different." We focus on who we are becoming. We commit to being in it for the long haul. We are going to give ourselves the time, the grace, and the permission to work through our mistakes. This is recovery. It's not about perfection; it's about progress.

Keep showing up and walking with God. Reorganize your priorities. Align yourself with extrinsic motivation if you have to, but realize that true change is intrinsic and lasting.

REFLECTIONS

MAKING PROGRESS IN OUR PLAN OF ACTION WILL REQUIRE THAT
WE SHOW UP, DO OUR PART, AND TRUST GOD WITH THE RESULTS.
IF WE FOCUS ON PROGRESS AND NOT PERFECTION, IT GIVES
US THE DETERMINATION WE NEED TO STAY THE COURSE.

1. Pretend that you failed at a task. What would you say to yourself about that failure?

2. How can you extend patience and compassion to yourself after a failure?

3. What would progress in that area look like? How can you put it into action?

GOING DEEPER . . .

Reflect on the progress that you have made so far on this journey. Write down some things that you are proud of yourself for and some new perspectives that you have about your life.

GIVING YOURSELF PERMISSION TO START AGAIN

In Day 28, I noted how John kept a membership at the YMCA but initially rarely used it. This is quite common. Many people start a workout program, but few actually maintain it. The key to success is to give ourselves permission to restart our programs the way that John did. This is a vital part of the process of change.

Let's say we are working out at the YMCA three days a week, but one week we miss a few days. Maybe we are sick or work takes us out of town. Then the following week other things come up, and before we know it, four weeks have gone by, and we haven't worked out at all. Now we're inactive again, and the inner critic begins to berate us for failing. But we're only failures if we stay inactive. Quitting is the only failure. John chose not to be a failure. He was inactive for many years, but he got back in the gym anyway. He reentered the process of change.

Dr. Patrick Carnes asks the question, "Why is recovery so hard?"[1] He believes one answer to this question is that recovery or change is about reclaiming integrity. It's about respecting ourselves enough to do the hard work of change. Sure, it's easier to be a couch potato than hit the gym three days a week. But laziness leads to a lack of self-respect, and it's hard to change if we don't respect ourselves enough to do so. Recovering from an inactive lifestyle means that we will have to reclaim integrity, and reclaiming integrity is about self-respect.

First, having self-respect begins when we accept ourselves as God sees us. When we accept ourselves, we understand that we may have to work on our faults. Hating ourselves ties one arm behind our back. Charles Reynolds Brown, dean of Yale Divinity School, once said, "Everyone is born into the world with a certain unrealized capacity. Let him accept his hand as it was dealt to him, and play the game, without wasting his time bemoaning the fact that his cards are not all aces and faces. Accept yourself for what you are, and for what, by the grace of God, you may yet become, and play the game."[2]

MIND

In the confrontation between the stream and the rock, the stream always wins—not through strength but by perseverance.
—H. JACKSON BROWN JR.

The Bible says that all of us should set aside everything that hinders and run the race that is set before us.[3] No one gets to choose his or her race. We don't get the opportunity to choose between being perfect and being imperfect. All of us are imperfect, and we'll remain that way until we die. The key is to "set aside" the things that are keeping us inactive in the process of change, such as laziness, self-defeating addictions, and listening to the inner critic that tells us that we will never change. These are the things that we've been discussing throughout the book, and these can't be defeated if we are divided against ourselves. We have to accept ourselves for who we are, and then work to become who, by the grace of God, He wants us to be. As the Serenity Prayer says, "God grant me the serenity to accept the things I cannot change, the courage to change the things I can, and wisdom to know the difference." This is a model prayer for self-acceptance.

Second, having self-respect means being ourselves in every situation.

Charles Reynolds Brown wrote, "Some people are hypocrites because they try to appear much better than they really are. Other people are hypocrites because, for some reason, they are afraid to allow that which is true and fine in them to be revealed."[4] The journey to freedom includes learning to be honest with ourselves. We stand in our own shoes. We speak from our own heart. We become true to ourselves and God. When we slip up, we get back up and continue our courageous battle to become true to ourselves.

BODY

Citing a study of ten thousand women ages forty to fifty-five, Miriam Nelson of Tufts University noted that 8 percent had difficulty doing simple physical tasks, such as climbing a flight of stairs, walking around a city block, or carrying a grocery bag. Frailty is going to catch up with these people in their fifties instead of their eighties or nineties. This is an epidemic of weakness that is especially occurring among American women and is happening in men, as well. We need strength training.

Third, having self-respect means living a life of humility. We understand and accept our limitations, the way that Muhammad Ali did as he was about to take off on an airplane flight. The stewardess reminded Ali, who was in his prime at the time, to fasten his seat belt. He shot back brashly, "Superman don't need no seat belt." The stewardess quickly replied, "Yeah, and Superman don't need no airplane, either." Ali humbly fastened his seat belt.

Understanding our limitations means that we realize that we're not Superman or Superwoman. We can't change our lives without God's help. This is true humility, as we've been learning. But sometimes we only accept God's help in certain areas of our lives. When we need help staying sober, we don't mind asking God for help. But we fail to depend on Him in our marriage or to help us become a better parent or to help us financially. We pick and choose areas where we allow God to help. But to get the type of life transformation that we need, we have to give God everything. We must come to the realization that change must happen at the core of who we are. This allows God to execute a plan of change by His strength. We do this by entering the process of transformation in our entire lives, instead of only in certain areas of our lives.

Think about washing a car. You would never wash only the hood of the car, leaving the remaining parts dirty. When you wash a car, you most likely complete the job by submitting the entire body of the car to the process. You don't choose the parts of the body that only the driver can see, such as the hood, and then deceive yourself into thinking that by washing only one area of the car you've made the entire car clean. It's the same when we submit our lives to God. Allowing Him to get us sober and keep us sober is only one area. To have a life of freedom, we have to subject all areas to God's help.

Fourth, gaining self-respect is a result of setting goals and achieving them. We feel good about ourselves when we achieve goals, so we should set some goals. Make them easy in the beginning. If you fail, start again. Get back up. If you need to lose weight, then set a goal to lose a pound a week and take the steps to achieve it—work out, walk, swim—do some type of activity. If you need to stop an addiction, then attend a twelve-step program once a week. This is a start, and sometimes all we need to get us going again is to take the first step. Give yourself permission to get back in the race.

There was once a man who knew how to restart after failure. When he was seven years old, his family was forced out of his home on a legal technicality, and he had to work to help support them. At age nine, his mother died. At twenty-two, he lost his job as a store clerk. He wanted to go to law school, but his education was lacking. At twenty-three, he went into debt to become a partner in a small store. At twenty-six, his business partner died, leaving him a huge debt that took him many years to repay. At twenty-eight, he asked his girlfriend of four years to marry him. She said no. At thirty-seven, on his third try, he was elected to Congress, but two years later, he failed to be reelected. At forty-one, his four-year-old son died. At forty-five, he ran for the Senate and lost. At forty-seven, he failed as the vice-presidential candidate. At forty-nine, he ran for the Senate again and lost. At fifty-one, he was elected the president of the United States. His name was Abraham Lincoln, a man whom many consider our greatest leader.

The one thing that remained constant throughout Lincoln's life was the way that he restarted after failure. He got back up. He set goals—he achieved some of them and failed at others. But he respected his ability enough to restart time and time again.

Self-respect begins when we accept ourselves with humility and truly become who God made us to be. We set goals and achieve them. We become something different and something better. If we slip up, we learn from it and move forward. The journey to freedom requires consistency and a willingness to run the race that is set before us, even if, like Abraham Lincoln, the race is littered with hurdles and past defeat.

REFLECTIONS

ACCEPT YOURSELF FOR WHO YOU ARE, AND FOR WHO,
BY THE GRACE OF GOD, YOU MAY YET BECOME.

1. What does having self-respect mean to you?

2. What does humility mean to you? How does it fit with self-respect?

3. What is one goal that you have set for yourself that you have yet to achieve? What is one step that you can take today toward achieving that goal?

GOING DEEPER . . .

Talk to God about the grace that He has bestowed upon you. Read Ephesians 2:1–10 to see just how much this grace abounds.

DESIRE TO BE SET FREE

In the movie *It's a Wonderful Life*, George Bailey longs to be successful and travel the world. He believes that monetary success will make him happy and content, and this becomes his goal and his passion. But through a chain of events, he never leaves Bedford Falls. He settles down, marries, and has what he believes is a mediocre career. He has friends and success, but not the type of success that he'd envisioned. He feels stuck in the small-town mode, away from the bright lights and the big city. Other friends have gone on to make lots of money and have accomplished great things, but George has remained in Bedford Falls.

George had originally been headed off to college when his father died, leaving him to run the family business. He is the faithful one who keeps the Bailey Savings and Loan afloat so that others can have affordable housing. Then enters the evil Mr. Potter, who is trying to buy the Savings and Loan and turn Bedford Falls into Pottersville. He steals money from George's absentminded uncle, and it looks as if George may have to go to jail. Everything falls apart, and he ends up on a bridge on Christmas Eve, ready to commit suicide. Then Clarence, George's guardian angel, takes him on a journey to look back at his life. George gets to see what life would have been like if he'd never been born. When he comes to the end of this journey with Clarence, we see him standing on the bridge looking down, saying, "Please, God, I want to live again." At the end of the movie, the people of Bedford Falls make a toast to George, "To the richest man in town!" This is how George Bailey discovers that true freedom is not found in money or status.

It's a Wonderful Life provides a great example of someone living in a self-made prison, because George doesn't have an addiction. He's not an alcoholic or dependent on any physical substances, but his internal life is dominated and controlled by an obsession to make money and see the world—to be different from his father. His happiness rests upon this fallacy to the point that he almost ends his life because of it.

SPIRIT

True life is lived when tiny changes occur.

—LEO TOLSTOY

We can become dependent on relationships, money, success, beauty, or fame—all because we are trying so hard not to feel lonely, poor, ugly, purposeless, or unsuccessful. This is why God warns us throughout the Bible to guard our hearts against false idols. False idols can take the place of an open relationship with Him, and becoming dependent on anything other than God builds a self-made prison. It's like being dependent on drugs or alcohol. Just as these substances put us in bondage, so does a focus on self and the acquisition of material possessions. As George Bailey discovered, money and status can never fully satisfy.

I've dealt with numerous George Bailey types at Restore—men and women who have become disillusioned with life. They came to Restore feeling like failures because they have failed to achieve their dreams, even though they were very successful by other standards. They had nice families and good friends, but they deceived themselves into believing that just because they hadn't reached a certain level of income they were failures. They believed that life had cheated them or passed them by, only to bless friends or neighbors with riches, beauty, fame, and good fortune. So, they had become bitter.

It's impossible to embrace and fully live in the present as long as we are trying to derive happiness from something outside of a relationship with God. Christ's mission is to set us free by turning our hearts to Him, instead of to materialism, addictions, or the approval of others. But it's hard to walk away from a life focused on self. We keep holding on because we are afraid of what will take its place. The path of least resistance is to hold on to what we have, even if it never sets our hearts free.

SPIRIT

I believe that God's basic nature is love. I don't think that we can even fathom the depth of what that really means. If love were like a substance that you could hold, that's what God would be.

—MIKE S. O'NEIL, *THE POWER TO CHOOSE*

We want all the benefits of the good life, and we set ourselves up for disappointment because many of us never achieve all of these things. We start our adult lives by saying something like, "I will be a millionaire by the time I'm thirty years old." And if we miss the mark, even though we have rich and endearing relationships and a comfortable lifestyle, we still feel like failures and become dissatisfied and bitter.

Sometimes it's easier to keep asking the question, "Why haven't I received riches and power?" than it is to move beyond it. Often, there is no logical answer to our questions. God has His reasons, but sometimes He doesn't choose to share them with us. This can be tough to deal with, but there is no easy answer other than to keep moving. Don't become bitter. Keep persevering. There's nothing wrong with having strong goals and a sense of ambition, but it is wrong to base our happiness on it. This is why Christ said, "If anyone would come after me, he must deny himself and take up his cross daily and follow me. For whoever wants to save his life will lose it, but whoever loses his life for me will save it."[1] Think about this when you feel trapped and bitter. Perhaps you are depending on all the wrong things to make you happy and fulfilled.

REFLECTIONS

FOR MANY PEOPLE, HAPPINESS IS CONTINGENT UPON MONEY, PRESTIGE, SUCCESS, OR RELATIONSHIPS.

1. It's impossible to embrace and fully live in the present as long as we are trying to derive happiness from something outside of a relationship with God. What are you holding on to from the past or the future that is keeping you from fully embracing the present?

2. What is really important to you? One way to know this is to think through what you would want people to say about you at your funeral. Write out what you would want friends, family, co-workers, and others to say about you.

GOING DEEPER . . .

Read Matthew 6:19–24 to see the treasures that are awaiting us in heaven. Write your thoughts in a journal.

FINISH STRONG

GRIEVING THE PAST SO YOU CAN REACH FOR THE FUTURE

One of my favorite *Twilight Zone* episodes is about someone who is trying to relive the past. A middle-aged businessman is working in a large metropolitan city. It's a dog-eat-dog atmosphere, and he's fighting to stay alive in the brutal competition. One day he gets into his car and aimlessly begins to drive. When he comes upon a small town, he parks his car and starts walking. As he's walking, he is shocked to realize that he's traveled back in time to his childhood. His old neighborhood is exactly as it was when he was a ten-year-old boy. And the weird *Twilight Zone* twist is that he runs into himself as a boy and calls out to himself. But the boy never hears him. Then he goes to his childhood home and tries to tell his father who he is and that he has traveled back in time, and they have a very moving conversation about how he wishes he could relive his childhood.

The story resonates with me because I know how this man feels. I, too, struggle with wanting to relive my youth. There is a powerful line in an old Christmas song that says, "Toyland, Toyland, little girl and boy land, but once you pass its borders you can never return again." But what this song doesn't tell us is that getting beyond the borders of our childhood may not happen with some people until well into adulthood. Sometimes actual chronological age has nothing to do with it. The *Twilight Zone* episode touches on this truth.

Stan experienced a similar breakthrough when he came to visit me at Restore. He told me everything over the course of an afternoon. He was on his fifth step in the twelve-step program, the step in which you sit down with one person and share your life story. It's called a "personal inventory." The goal is to answer these types of questions: "Why do I drink? Why do I seek out pornography? Why do I feel rage? Why do I have such a negative self-image? Why am I the way I am?"

MIND

Fill your mind with the thought that God is there. And once your mind is truly filled with that thought, when you experience difficulties, it will be as easy as breathing for you to remember, "My heavenly Father knows all about this!"

—OSWALD CHAMBERS, MY UTMOST FOR HIS HIGHEST

Stan told me about how he grew up with an alcoholic father. He desperately desired his father's love, but his father never expressed affection. Instead, he was mean and prone to fits of rage. One evening when Stan was ten years old, he felt an overwhelming compulsion to go put his arms around his father and tell him how much he loved him. He mustered up the courage, went to his father, put his arms around him, and said, "Dad, I love you." His father pushed him away and said, "What's up with you? Leave me alone." So, Stan never tried again.

Because of his relationship with his father, Stan felt insignificant and unworthy of love his whole life. As he told his story, it became evident that I was not talking to a sixty-year-old man, but a ten-year-old boy who was still longing for his father's love and yet was still feeling unworthy of it.

We need to rescue our hearts from the past. We do this by expressing grief. We work through the grief by feeling the pain. Cloud and Townsend write, "Our past losses and hurts can be healed as we allow ourselves to attach to them the sadness that's warranted. Simply put, we need to grieve. It's a critical step in God's process for healing hurt."[1] Letting go to reach for the future means that we must stop trying to relive the past. Sometimes we relive the past because it was safe back then. It was joyful and carefree, with no responsibilities or problems.

For twenty-five years, I had the same recurring dream. In my dream, I'm in junior high school, the most joyful period of my life. I'm a young teenager riding bikes with my friends, free to roam wherever I want, to play games and laugh. I had no huge responsibilities; it was a time of innocence and play. I had all these great dreams of what I was going to do with my life, about what I was going to be. Everything seemed plausible. Most of my life was still ahead of me. But in my dream, I'm walking around the school checking doors, peeping through the windows into the gym, wanting so much to get inside, but the doors are locked. I would wake up from the dream and feel an incredible sense of sadness and longing.

We usually think of experiencing a loss as when someone dies, but the loss of dreams can also trigger a time of mourning. Longing and thirsting to go back, just like the man in the *Twilight Zone* episode, I wanted to find that twelve-year-old boy so I could tell him not to waste his life. I guess it was because I felt that I had so much hope back then, with no failures to speak of. But as I became an adult, my addictions and divorce left me fragile. Maybe these experiences left me longing for a more innocent time.

I never dealt with my grief until I entered a grief counseling class to be certified to help families at the YMCA. In this class, I found myself working through my own grief, and this is when I realized just how much I'd lost back then. But then I realized that at the end of lost hopes and dreams is Christ. That's the good news. The good news is that He gives new beginnings. We may not be able to relive the past, but we can begin again as we grieve the past and let it go. This is why I don't have that dream anymore. The Lord has given me a new dream, a new vision, and a new purpose.

A friend once told me that early in our lives we only know how to get things—but we don't learn how to let go. As we move through our journey to freedom, many of us need to look into our lives and move through the process of grief as we let go and complete the losses of our lives. Then we will be able to dream new dreams and begin to embrace the wonderful gift of Christ's promise, "With God all things are possible."[2]

In an earlier chapter, I mentioned the phrase "the darkness of the beginning." In our darkest moment, the most important decision we will make is to reach out for God and ask Him to heal our hurts. The best part of life can start now. The new beginning will grow from the fertile ashes of past destruction. In this soil, God's power is made possible because we realize that our strength is ashes and only God has the ability to take our past destruction and use it for good. There's a great verse in the Bible that says, "We know that in everything God works for the good of those who love him."[3]

The journey to freedom is about new beginnings. Wherever you are, whatever your age, wherever you've been, the best part of your life begins now. It did for Stan. He grieved and moved beyond the borders of his sad childhood. I grieved the loss of my joyful childhood and embraced a new adulthood. This final week is about taking the journey. Reach out and make these last days count. Let this encouragement propel you along in the process of change.

REFLECTIONS

WE NEED TO GRIEVE KEY HURTS AND LOSSES SO SOMETHING NEW CAN BEGIN IN OUR LIVES. WE NEED GOD'S HEALING FOR OUR HEARTS.

1. What are some of the different types of loss that you can experience in your lifetime (outside of loss caused by death)?

2. What loss have you had in your life that you have been unable to grieve fully? What have you done with it until now?

3. What steps do you need to take to begin grieving that loss in order to be able to move forward?

GOING DEEPER . . .

Read John 16:20–24 and meditate on what new things can be brought out from your current situation.

TAKE A RISK:
STEP OUT OF THE BOAT

It was sometime after midnight when Jesus sent His disciples across the lake. Jesus needed time alone with the Father. Reluctant to leave Him, the disciples pushed their boats into the water. Later, a storm began to brew in the far corner of the lake; then a light storm became a squall. The wind flapped the sails; the choppy water smacked the hull. And then, a strange thing happened: it seemed as if there was a ghost approaching them, walking on the water. As Christ approached the boat, He could see their frightened stances. But Christ said, "Have courage! It is I. Do not be afraid."[1]

Most of us would have been relieved and invited Him into the boat. But Peter, the adventurous one, wanted to walk on the water, too. He called to Christ, "Lord, if it is really you, then command me to come to you on the water." Christ said, "Come."[2] So, Peter stepped out.

The riskiest step of any new venture is always the first step. It's the bravest, too. Take Peter, for example. Our logic and understanding of the scientific rules of this world tell us that we can't walk on water because a human weighs more than water. It is a scientific fact that the human will sink. But sometimes we have to defy our logic and understanding. So why don't we take that first risky step to change? Often, it's because we don't want to let go of the familiar. Change breaks the rules; something different happens. This fear is what keeps us in the boat, where we are comfortable.

To change anything in our lives, risk will be involved. Changing deeply ingrained habits, destructive patterns, and addictions requires great risk. Every day we are involved in activities of risk. Consider these facts:

- Automobiles cause 20 percent of all fatalities.
- Trains, planes, and boats cause 16 percent of accidents.
- Walking near roads and highways causes 15 percent of all accidents.
- Household accidents make up 17 percent of all accidents.[3]

If we attempted to stay away from these areas, we would not travel at all; it would be too risky. But each day we push out into a world of the unknown, where anything can happen.

SPIRIT

It is within my power either to serve God or not to serve Him. Serving Him, I add to my own good in the good of the whole world. Not serving Him, I forfeit my own good and deprive the world of that good which was in my power to create.

—LEO TOLSTOY

The first step is always the hardest. Notice that Peter stepped toward Christ. Peter needed Christ's power and His strength. Courage empowers us as we trust the One toward whom we are stepping. The courage for our first step will come from moving toward Christ, as well. We need His power and grace to do for us what we cannot do for ourselves. What is impossible for you or me alone is possible with Christ, for all things are possible with Him. When Jesus said, "Come," Peter believed and walked toward Christ.

But then, Peter made the mistake of taking his focus off of Christ. He allowed the storm to distract him. Likewise, we often take our eyes off of the solution in front of us and concentrate on the negative circumstances. We begin to believe that we can't overcome, and we begin to sink. Notice that, when Peter began to sink, he made an important choice. He reached out for Christ's hand.

Many times we're like the young boy who was doing his best to lift a large rock. He grunted and puffed as he tried various methods for lifting the rock, but in spite of all of his efforts, the rock wouldn't budge. His father walked by, and after watching his son's struggle for a few moments, asked if he was having trouble. The boy answered, "Yes, I've tried everything, and it won't move." The father replied, "Are you sure that you have tried every possibility, that you have used every resource at your disposal?" The boy looked up with frustration and grunted out a "Yes!" With kindness, the father bent over and softly said, "No, my son, you haven't. You haven't asked for my help."

Many times, we try lifting things that are too heavy for us. We exhaust our strength. We become frustrated and defeated when all we had to do was ask for Christ's help. He reaches out through people, groups, or a team at work, and all we have to do is grab His hand. If you try to stand alone, you will sink.

Peter had an incredible experience with Christ when he walked on the water. All day, every day, we have opportunities to experience Christ, to step out and trust Him. We only need to build into our schedule appointed times to meet with Him.

One of Rabbi Ben Jochai's pupils once asked why God hadn't furnished the children of Israel enough manna in the desert to last for a full year. The rabbi used a parable to supply the answer. He said, "Once there was a king who had a son to whom he gave a yearly allowance, paying him the entire sum on a fixed date. It soon happened that the day on which the allowance was due was the only day of the year when the father ever saw his son. So the king changed his plan and gave his son day-by-day that which was sufficient for the day; then the son visited his father every morning. How he needed his father's unbroken love, companionship, wisdom, and giving!"[4]

Our journey to freedom begins when we accept the risk and take the first step. We remain focused, but if we slip, we grab His hand. Storms will occur. Old feelings of remorse, low self-esteem, and doubt will cause distractions, but remember the One who is in the storm with you. Reach out and take His hand.

REFLECTIONS

TO CHANGE ANYTHING IN OUR LIVES, RISK WILL BE INVOLVED.

1. When have you taken a risk? What happened?

2. What "boat" do you need to get out of in order to change?

3. What can you do on a daily basis to put your focus on Christ and
    reach out to Him in order to get out of this boat?

GOING DEEPER . . .

*Read Lamentations 3:22–26 and think through some ways that you can seek
God daily.*

PERSEVERANCE: THE STRENGTH TO FINISH THE RACE

Thomas Edison gave us some wise thoughts regarding perseverance. The famous inventor made thousands of trial runs and prototypes before he finally got the lightbulb to operate. One day, he gave a workman a task, but the man responded, "Mr. Edison, it cannot be done."

Edison said, "How often have you tried?"

"About two thousand times."

"Go back and try two thousand more; you have only found that there are two thousand ways in which it cannot be done."

Edison also said, "Genius is one-percent inspiration and ninety-nine-percent perspiration."[1]

Most of us have an aversion to any type of pain or discomfort. We try a few times to change, then we give up when it doesn't seem to work. We live in this "microwave generation" where we want everything fixed right now. We believe that discomfort is a sin.

The Bible says, "My brethren, count it all joy when you fall into various trials, knowing that the testing of your faith produces perseverance."[2] We don't think about having joy in a trial. We think, "How can I get out of this painful predicament?" No one gets up in the morning and says, "Where can I find a trial today? I want to test my faith."

God is not sadistic, nor does He think that we should be sadistic people and go about punishing ourselves. He desires growth in our soul, and He knows that sticking with the pain and discomfort of some of our circumstances teaches us patience. We learn to endure because it leads to victory. That's why we are told to count it all joy whenever we face trials.

I remember how much I hated summer practice as a high school and college football player. We were out in the ninety-degree weather twice a day. Sweat poured from every pore in our bodies. When someone tackled us and plowed us into the ground, sweat flew off us like throwing a soaked sponge at a wall. No one enjoyed practice season. We wanted to get to the games. We wanted to play an opponent under the bright lights of the stadium. We learned that if we could endure practice and weight training, we'd get the incredible reward of playing in a game. And when we got to the game, we discovered that all of the practicing gave us the strength and confidence to be successful. Later on, I realized how much the game of football taught me about life.

Life is much like an athletic event or a race. Life requires perseverance to see it through, especially when we are trying to change bad habits or addictions. So count it as joy when you have to face down an addiction every day, because the victory over the addiction is shaping your soul one small step at a time. Anyone who wins the battle of weight management can tell you that it came off one pound at a time. We accomplish any goal by persevering through small steps. Think of Dave Ramsey, the financial guru. At one time, he went bankrupt. Now he's a best-selling author, telling others how to manage their finances. Ask him how he did it, and he'll tell you that it was through perseverance. He attacked one bill at a time until he got it paid. Then he did the same thing with the next one.

Passion comes from purpose. Richard Leider writes, "Purpose is the conscious choice of what, where, and how to make a positive contribution to our world. It is the theme, quality, or passion we choose to center our lives around. Once we discover our gifts and what moves us, the whole world takes on a new energy. Our life becomes a thing of spiritual significance."[3] This is why it's important to find our purpose in the world. Our life needs a theme and a reason, and once we discover that, it will be the force behind perseverance. Without passion, life becomes drudgery.

BODY

Some of the benefits of strength training include replacing fat with muscle, which in turn increases strength and energy, as well as improving balance and flexibility and boosts metabolism, a key to permanent weight loss by as much as 15 percent. Strength training also has had an impact, on numerous medical conditions; it strengthens the heart, relieves arthritis symptoms, lifts depression, and prevents or reverses the bone loss commonly known as osteoporosis.

—MIRIAM NELSON

Patience is the main ingredient for perseverance. The Bible says, "But let patience have its perfect work, that you may be perfect and complete, lacking nothing."[4] Anything worth achieving, any struggle or challenge, requires patience. We don't plant a garden, and then expect a crop overnight. We give the invisible time to become visible. The Bible says, "A farmer patiently waits for his valuable crop to grow from the earth and for it to receive the autumn and spring rains. You, too, must be patient. Do not give up hope."[5]

We can plant healthy habits, but we must not expect instant results. Persevere with patience, knowing that in due time your new healthy habits will produce a crop of rewards. Addictions become easier to resist. The pounds will come off. Destructive patterns lose their grip. But it won't happen unless we are patient. Another verse in the Bible states, "we also glory in tribulations, knowing that tribulation produces perseverance; and perseverance, character; and character, hope" (Rom. 5:3–4 NKJV). It's a natural progression.

Francie Larrieu Smith competed in her fifth Olympic event as a marathon hopeful at the age of thirty-nine. In a *Sports Illustrated* article, she spoke about a race: "That's what gives me the old hope, if I can see the finish line I can always find something."[6] When we see the finish line, we can muster up the strength to get there.

When everything in us says to just lie down and quit, we can draw from God the strength to finish. To persevere, let patience have time to work. The Bible says, "And let us not grow weary while doing good, for in due season we shall reap if we do not lose heart."[7]

REFLECTIONS

ANY TIME WE TRY TO CHANGE SOMETHING,
WE CAN EXPECT SOME LEVEL OF DISCOMFORT.

1. How can your perseverance develop strong character?

2. In what situation have you experienced the joy that comes through trial and perseverance?

3. What would getting a glimpse of your finish line mean to you?

GOING DEEPER . . .

Read Hebrews 12:1–3 to see how we can persevere through trials.

THE STRUGGLE FOR FREEDOM

A reporter once asked advice columnist Ann Landers what question she received the most. In response, Ann said that the most common question is, "What's wrong with me?"

We hear this question on a continual basis at Restore. People feel broken, have little hope that things will change, and just want to know what's wrong with them. This is why it's essential for those in recovery or healing to hear the voice of Christ speaking through the ages, "Come to me, all of you who are tired and have heavy loads, and I will give you rest."[1] We should go to Him just as we are. We should go, fully aware of what little we have to offer and knowing that His love will drive out the fears caused by our addictions and destructive habits.

People who come to Restore usually aren't seeking God. They want to change and improve their lifestyle, their health, and their relationships. They want the pain to stop. But soon they discover that their dilemma is not only physical or emotional, but also spiritual. When they realize this, then they are ready to hear God calling them to a place of safety where they can lay down their burdens. Their problem leads them to God. It's much like what bees go through to ensure the healthy development of their young. The queen lays each egg in a six-sided cell filled with enough pollen and honey to feed the egg until it reaches a certain stage of maturity. Then the queen bee seals the capsule with wax. When the occupant exhausts its supply of nourishment, the tiny creature emerges from its confinements. But it wrestles, tussles, and strains to get through the wax seal. And in the agony of its exit, the bee rubs off the membrane that encases its wings—so that when it does emerge, it is able to fly.

SPIRIT

> To worship is to quicken the conscience by the holiness of God, to feed the mind with the truth of God, to purge the imagination by the beauty of God, to open the heart to the love of God, and to devote the will to the purpose of God.
> —SIR WILLIAM TEMPLE

When I hit bottom, I wanted God to take away the pain. Then I understood God's invitation and slowly I began to turn homeward toward Him. I realized that my journey was no longer about stopping the pain or having a better life, even though it ended up being a new life. I discovered that an incredibly loving God had captured my heart. He transformed my desires and every aspect of my life by loving me, guiding me, comforting me, nurturing me, encouraging me, and supporting me. I came to a place where my burdens fell away and I entered into a loving relationship with Him.

HOW TO LOVE GOD IN RETURN

We know that relationships aren't one-sided. If they were, they wouldn't last long. The part that we play in a relationship with God is much like a marriage. In a marriage relationship, we should live for what's best for the relationship. Therefore, we do our best not to become involved in behavior that damages that mutual love and understanding. If we have ongoing affairs in our marriage, then the relationship will shatter. No one wants to stay married to someone who can't be faithful. And this is what God wants from us. He desires faithfulness in our covenant.

Once we begin a relationship with God, it should not be based on God's wrath or on our fear of Him. The Bible says, "Where God's love is, there is no fear, because God's perfect love drives out fear. It is punishment that makes a person fear, so love is not made perfect in the person who fears."[2]

Many times, I've fled out of fear and searched for something familiar that offered safety. I thought that my addictions provided safety, but they only put me in further bondage and fear. Most of the time, we don't realize that our addictions and dependencies only deepen our fear. In this bondage, we feel as though God would never want a relationship with us. We feel tainted and end up wandering for many years through our lives searching for love.

BODY

Last but not least, it is essential to have a measure of anticipation and joy for whatever exercise or activity you choose to take on. Your physical exertion needs to delight you in some way, or it simply will not become a consistent part of your life.

—RUTH MCGINNIS, *THE GOOD LIFE*

Dr. Gerald May writes, "For the power of addiction to be overcome, human will must act in concert with divine will. The human spirit must flow with the Holy Spirit. Personal power must be aligned with the power of grace. . . . The alignment of our will with God's must happen at a heart level, through authentic choices of faith that are empowered by God."[3] We can't defeat addiction on our own, nor can we turn everything over to God and expect Him to do all the work for us.

We must still choose an authentic faith and trust Him with all of our hearts, taking one step at a time. My efforts to change are no longer about just using God to get what I want, but something much deeper. I dedicate and devote everything in my life to a loving relationship with God, and everything flows from this central relationship.

I will definitely struggle through the pain at first. But as I do, God works through the pain to do something to my soul. I am being transformed.

REFLECTIONS

A SPIRITUAL DILEMMA IS JUST AS REAL
AS PHYSICAL AND EMOTIONAL TURMOIL.

1. Have your problems caused you to move toward God or away from Him?

2. What are your thoughts on the process of the bee in this chapter? What could be the role of pain and struggle in your life?

3. Are you ready to allow God to do His work in your life? Explain why or why not.

GOING DEEPER . . .

Read and meditate on Galatians 5:1 and Matthew 11:28–29 to get a glimpse of the freedom that Christ has to offer.

BLUEPRINT TO FREEDOM: DESIGNING YOUR PERSONAL PLAN FOR CHANGE

Today you will design a Personal Plan of Change. You will set goals in the three areas of change that we've discussed—spirit, mind, and body. After defining these goals, you will write out the steps that it will take to achieve these goals. Finally, you will put together your "Freedom Team," which consists of the key people who will walk with you along the journey to freedom. They will provide direction, support, encouragement, inspiration, and accountability to help you accomplish your plan of action.

SAMPLE PERSONAL PLAN OF CHANGE

Step 1: Write out a brief personal assessment of where you are in body, mind, and spirit.

My name is Stan. I am fifty years old. I am twenty pounds overweight and have been inactive since college. Every year I've made New Year's resolutions to lose weight, but I never stick to them. I also have a highly stressful job. I have not been sleeping well, and I know that my eating habits are poor. My alcohol intake has increased over the years, and now I have begun to think about alcohol during the day. When my wife goes to bed, I sometimes sit and drink alone. I'm starting to realize that I haven't thought about having a spiritual life for years. I have become obsessed with the past and the mistakes that I've made. I often wake up with a headache and become anxious when I think about going to work. What's wrong with me?

Step 2: Write out your goals.
Spirit: Reconnect with God and develop a daily relationship with Him.

Mind: Reduce stress levels and begin to feel a sense of relaxation apart from alcohol. Begin to feel a sense of joy, peace, and contentment with life.

Body: Lose twenty pounds by exercising.

Step 3: Write out specific steps to meet your goals.
Spirit: Will get up thirty minutes earlier in the morning and have quiet time reading *My Utmost for His Highest* by Oswald Chambers, and the related Bible verses. Will begin a journal with prayers and thoughts.

Mind: Will join my friend Bob and attend a Christ-centered twelve-step group at my church.

Body: Will join a local YMCA and get set up on personal fitness. Will work out four days a week in the morning after my quiet time.

Step 4: Find a support team.
Support Community:
Ten-step group; men's group at church
Individual Support:
Bob; sponsor or accountability partner from twelve-step group; pastor at my church; Steve from office as a workout partner

Step 5: Write a brief description of exactly what your life will be like when this change occurs.

There will be a peacefulness that settles in on my life that is not manufactured through any form of mood-altering drug such as alcohol. I will have a personal relationship with God that is the foundational relationship of everything in my life. I will be a better husband and father. I will enjoy my life and my work, seeing it as a part of a greater purpose. Physically, I will have more energy and less stress. Through all of this, I will sleep better, I will feel better, I will look better. I'm looking forward to having a zest for life that has been missing over the past years.

Step 6: Write out a daily prayer to use as you walk the journey to freedom.

Dear God, thank You for this day. Thank You for loving me. I pray that Your love overflows into my life and that my life will abound with hope and joy. Give me the strength and courage to follow through to the best of my ability with this plan for today. Guide me into Your will in all that I do. Amen.

Step 7: Share this plan with at least one person from your support team list within the first week.

YOUR PERSONAL ACTION PLAN

Step 1: Write out a brief personal assessment of where you are in body, mind, and spirit.

Step 2: Write out your goals in the space provided below. For example, if you desire a closer walk with God, then write this in the *Spirit* category below. If you want to learn how to renew your mind by not allowing the inner critic to control you, then write that in the *Mind* category. If you want to lose weight, write that in the *Body* category.

Spirit:

Mind:

Body:

Step 3: Write out specific steps to meet your goals. (Hint: go back to the last question on each day of your journey and use your answers to help formulate your plan.)

Spirit:
Example: attend church regularly; spend ten minutes a day in prayer

Mind:
Example: begin a twelve-step program; contact a therapist

Body:
Example: walk thirty minutes daily; increase fruits and vegetables in my diet; decrease sweets and fats; lift weights three times a week

Step 4: Find a support team. Find a support community. (Choose one of the options below or another group that suits your needs.)

Restore Ministries—http://www.restoreymca.org or
    www.journeytofreedom.org
Alcoholics Anonymous—http://www.alcoholics-anonymous.org/
Overeaters Anonymous—http://www.oa.org/index.htm
Sexaholics Anonymous—http://www.saa-recovery.org/
Al Anon—http://www.al-anon.org/
Narcotics Anonymous—http://www.na.org/
Bible Study/Church Small Group:
Other:

Find individuals to support you. (List some individuals below who can support you in your journey.)

Friend:

Sponsor:

Therapist:

Counselor:

Doctor:

Pastor:

Life Coach:

Personal Trainer:

Nutritionist:

Physical Therapist:

Step 5: Write a brief description of exactly what your life will be like when this change occurs.

Step 6: Write out a daily prayer to use as you walk the journey to freedom.

Step 7: Share this plan with at least one person from your support team list within the first week.

PERSONAL COMMITMENT TO THE ACTION PLAN: YOU CAN DO IT!

The first step of our journey together is wrapping up. We've learned how the change process works, how motivation must be intrinsic to produce change, and that the power to overcome rests in a loving relationship with God. We've learned that we can't make it alone. We need others on this journey. We realize that God has a plan for each step of the way, loving us, strengthening us, encouraging us, and doing for us what we cannot do for ourselves.

Now we approach a very critical point on the journey to freedom. Below is a review of what we've learned. Use it as a reference throughout your journey to gauge your growth and to remember the key points of our study together. You may want to review this list each day.

In this journey, you will need a commitment to live by, as well as something that helps you remember your commitment. On the next page you will find a list of keys for success in your process of change, and a place for you to sign that you are ready to begin your journey. The journey to real change starts with your signature. For accountability, ask a friend or mentor to sign along with you. Ask them to hold you accountable to this commitment. You're on your way to a lifetime of health, hope, and happiness!

KEYS TO THE SUCCESS OF MY PERSONAL PLAN OF CHANGE

- Maintain an attitude of humility and honesty.
- Don't focus on the problems in the past or perfection for the future. Focus on one day at a time and making the right choices.
- Give yourself permission to get started again on your plan if you slip up, but don't stay in that destructive pattern. If you have no commitment to the plan, then admit it and wait until you're ready to begin.
- Treat yourself with compassion. Learn to be gentle with yourself. Don't internalize mistakes with negative self-talk. Go to God. Go to people on your team. Get the support and affirmation that you need to get back on the plan.
- Learn from your mistakes. What are they teaching you? What can you do to avoid these slipups in the future? Let your mistakes be a teaching tool, not a condemning device.
- Avoid isolation. Our strengths are in numbers, in staying connected to our team and community. Isolation is a dangerous place. None of us has the strength to make it alone.
- Change is a process that takes time. Our journeys will take time. Be patient with yourself.
- Remember, consistency and time equal change. Take things one day at a time. The new and improved behaviors will eventually come.
- Don't make emotional decisions. Use common sense.
- Don't be discouraged if it seems that you aren't making any progress. Many people quit because they feel that they're not changing. Don't make any overall decisions about your growth until you are thirty to sixty days into your plan of action. Sometimes it takes three or four tries before our plan finally sticks. Again, just keep showing up. Keep coming back and working the plan. The only way you can suffer defeat is by quitting.
- Remember, in the end, it's all about coming back to God and resting in His strength through His grace. He will take care of you.

Dear God,

I, _____, promise, with Your help and with unwavering determination, to follow through with my plan of change to the best of my ability. God, give me strength and courage. Thank You for Your grace and mercy. May Your love encourage me along the way, and remind me to walk this out one day at a time as I focus on my relationship with You. Amen.

[Sign your name]

[Signed by a member of your freedom team, friend, or spouse]

Congratulations, you are on your way to a life of freedom!

We would love to hear from you about your journey. Visit us at our Web site, www.journeytofreedom.org, and share your story with us and continue your journey. God bless you!

TIPS FOR LEADING A JOURNEY TO FREEDOM SMALL GROUP

Welcome and thank you for accepting the challenge of leading others along their own journeys to freedom. These tips are designed to aid you in creating a small group setting that is productive and full of hope, health, and happiness.

PREPARATION

Being well prepared will help alleviate any anxiety you may have about leading your group. When you know what you want to accomplish in your group, it will help you stay on track with the lesson plan. Plus, if you're not prepared, participants will pick up on your lack of preparation, which might affect their own dedication to the group and the process of change. In extreme cases, lack of preparation may even cause you to lose some participants. If the leader is not committed, why should the participants be committed? So come to your group prepared to lead them.

Be a role model. A good facilitator is simply a model group participant. Be on time. Be prepared. Do your homework. Guard against moodiness. Be consistent. Be positive. Be a good listener. Maintain confidentiality. Be enthusiastic.

Recognize your limitations. It is important that you remember that you are not responsible for the results of your group. You are not responsible to "fix" anyone. You are not a counselor, a therapist, or a minister. You are a mentor, one who is helping guide another down a path that you have traveled before. Each participant is responsible for his or her own growth, journey, and life.

Pace the group. Use gentleness and patience as you pace the progress of the group. Rushing through the lessons might be exhausting for your participants. Try to find some kind of meaningful devotional, excerpt from a book, or song to emphasize and complement what you are studying.

Also, *watch the pace of the sharing.* If some members are opening up and sharing for long periods of time, try not to let their problems control the group. Tell them, "I would love to continue this discussion with you after the meeting." Then say, "Will that be OK?" This will keep you from appearing uncaring and will give the group permission to get back on track.

Plan your time so that you are able to get through the majority of the recommended questions, but settle for quality of questions and answers over quantity. The goal is to have a productive meeting. Getting through every question in the lesson may seem optimal, but it may not accomplish the goal.

SKILLS FOR SMALL GROUP

Avoid being the center of attention. Your role as leader is to get the group involved in sharing, to keep the discussion topic moving forward, and to make sure that your group is on time. Be sure that the necessary material is covered. You are there to give direction and guidance to the group, so avoid dominating the group by talking too much in the sessions. Focus on being a facilitator.

Be aware of your group. As a facilitator, get to know your group members. In order to help them as much as possible, you need to be aware and in tune with their needs. Pay attention to the members' body language, their actions, and what they are saying and sharing. Assess each participant in their responses and in their openness (or lack of).

Don't let one member dominate the group. Handling the "talker" in your group will require some skill. Be careful, because if one member begins to dominate your group, it can alienate some of the more reserved members. In order to handle this person in your group, think about positioning. Sit beside the individual instead of across from him to avoid prolonged eye contact. When presenting a question or topic for discussion, put a time limit on member's responses. If someone runs over the limit, don't be afraid to break in and praise his or her point, but then raise a new question back to the group about what they have shared. Validate the individual's feelings and input, but then focus the discussion. If needed, confront the person in private outside of the group and let him know that he may be dominating conversation, but never embarrass him in front of the whole group.

Allow silence. Often facilitators can become uncomfortable with silence in group discussion. Sometimes it is good to have a moment of silence so that the participants will speak up and start owning the conversation. Do not feel that you have to fill the void. If the group members think that you are going to fill the silence, then they will learn to wait for you. If you find that there has been a considerable amount of time given to answer a question and no one is speaking up, you might ask them why they are silent or move on to another question.

Contain the desire to rescue. If someone gets emotionally upset or begins to cry and show emotion during the session, avoid anything that could interfere with the member feeling the emotion of the moment. Let him or her express the emotions and deal with them, even if they are painful. While they are sharing do not reach over and hug them, touch them, or comfort them. After he or she has finished sharing and is done, then offer a hug if you desire. Thank and affirm the person for his courage.

Use self-disclosure appropriately. One element of being a good facilitator is a willingness to be vulnerable and to share your journey of change in the appropriate times. However, be careful that you do not use the group to deal with your unresolved issues.

Guide the Discussion. As you lead, consistently state and reiterate the boundaries of discussion: confidentiality, respect, and the right to pass. Accept what each person has to say without making sudden judgments. Be the primary catalyst toward providing a warm, open, trusting, and caring atmosphere. This will help the group gradually take ownership.

CLOSING THE GROUP

Manage the time wisely. It is important that your group start and end on time. Strive for consistency, beginning in the first meeting by starting and ending on time and continuing that schedule each week.

SESSION ONE: INTRODUCTION WEEK

Lesson Goal:

In your first meeting you will not cover any material. You will begin to get to know each other as a group and learn the structure and guidelines for the next seven weeks as well as the expectations of each participant.

Leading the Session:

- Welcome the participants and commend them on taking this action to pursue change in their lives.
- Ask each participant to share whatever information they are comfortable sharing about themselves with the group. Name, occupation, number and ages of children and/or grandchildren, where you were born, how you heard of this group, etc., are good places to start. Be sure that you and your co-facilitator (if applicable) introduce yourselves first to increase their comfort level.
- Show the first session of Scott Reall's video (if applicable) and talk about what they have to look forward to as a group in the upcoming eight weeks.
- Present group guidelines to the participants:
  1. Confidentiality is of the utmost importance.
  2. Group members are not required to talk but encouraged to do so.
  3. Agree to accept each other and to encourage one another.
  4. Do not give advice, "fix," or try to rescue other group members.
  5. Be honest.
  6. Be on time.

7. Agree to make the weekly meetings and the daily work a priority.

8. Ask if anyone would like to ask a question or add a group guideline.

   - The goal is for participants to feel safe, secure, and encouraged.

- Choose one of the following warm-up questions to open up the group and begin to break the ice.

   1. What do you like to do when you have free time?

   2 What is a special talent or skill that you possess?

   3. Tell us about a wonderful experience you have had in your life.

- Pair your group up into couples, and give each person five minutes to answer the following questions.

   1. What brought you here today?

   2. What is it in your life you want to change?

   3. What excuses will you give yourself to not come to group or do your homework?

Closing the Group:

- Encourage the group members to come back to the next meeting.

- Encourage group members to read all of Days 1–6 and answer the questions at the end of each day and to write their answers in the blank space provided. Tell them to come next week ready to discuss their responses.

- Explain to them the *Going Deeper* questions and challenges at the end of each day. They are for further reflection and Bible study.

- Assign accountability partners for each participant and, if possible, pair them with the partner that they were paired with for the last exercise. Ask them to exchange phone numbers and e-mail addresses.

Accountability Partner Guidelines:

1. Discuss the specifics of the change they're trying to achieve.

2. Relate how they are doing in spirit, mind, and body.

3. Ask their partner about their struggles, problems, and particular difficulties.

4. Be considerate of each other's time and situations, and remember that the purpose is to discuss change. Make an effort to take the conversation beyond a superficial level.

The Importance of Accountability Partners:

One of the best tools to help us through the rough times in our journey to freedom is accountability. Often we don't realize how much accountability has influenced and affected our decisions throughout our lives. We are accountable to get to work on time or we may lose our jobs. In school, athletes have to keep their grades up, attend class, and get to practice or they are off the team. In the same way, unless we have some sort of accountability, many of us will not sustain our efforts to change. We need accountability to develop the discipline of sticking with something, especially if it's new to us.

- Be sure to thank them for coming this week. Express how excited you are to be with them and to discover where this journey is going to take all of you as a group.
- Close with prayer, singing, the serenity prayer, or any other positive way that you feel is appropriate.

SESSION TWO: STARTING YOUR JOURNEY TO FREEDOM

Lesson Goal:

This session and this week's reading are about learning how to contemplate change. Participants will learn that changing their lives first begins when they realize that change is possible. The group should define its purpose, which is to help one another contemplate change. You may want to read this definition of contemplation to the group:

Contemplation: A deep spiritual and mental thought whereby we struggle to understand our problems and their causes so that we can begin to seek possible solutions.

Leading the Session:

- Review guidelines for a smooth small group session.
- After a brief check-in, ask participants to share anything from this week that they felt moved by or that they thought was important to share.

Here are questions from this week that we want you to focus on.

- What does hope mean to you? (Day 1 question 1)
- When have you lost all hope of changing? (Day 2 question 1)
- Why do we have a hard time letting go of some things even when we know they are bad for our lives? (Day 3 question 2)
- Why do addictions never fulfill our longings to love and to be loved? How has this been true in your life? (Day 4 question 3)
- Reflect on the dragon story. If God were to peel off the "dragon skin" of your false self, what would you find? (Day 6 question 2)
- What feelings have you been avoiding or suppressing because you are afraid of the pain that comes with them? How can we allow our feelings to help us instead of hurt us? (Day 5 questions 1 & 2)
- If there is time, see if anyone is willing to share from their Going Deeper times.
- Encourage group members to read all of Days 7–12 and answer the questions at the end of each day in the blank spaces provided. Ask them to come next week prepared to discuss.
- Finally, thank everyone for coming and close by reading Psalm 139 to the group.

SESSION 3: HIDDEN PRISONS: LIFE-CONTROLLING ISSUES

Lesson Goal:

In this week, we are going to look at the impact that fears, insecurities, and negative thoughts have on our lives. We will discuss why we

sink into denial and blame others for our problems. We'll learn to recognize how we've developed patterns of response to negative thoughts
and fears. The goal for this week is to eradicate negative, self-destructive
thoughts that have developed into permanent and very deeply entrenched behaviors. We will begin to look at how we can move from a
place of anxiety to a place of peace.

Leading the Session:

- Review guidelines for a smooth small group session.
- Facilitate a brief check-in of the week and possible feelings check.
- Focus on these questions for this week's lesson:
  - How has fear influenced your attempts to change? (Day 8
    question 1)
  - How would you live differently if you weren't afraid? (Day 8
    question 3)
  - What are the negative thoughts about yourself that you struggle
    with? What are some of the truths that you came up with from
    Romans 8 and Zephaniah 3:17 to counter these thoughts? (Day
    10 question 1 and Day 10 Going Deeper)
  - How do you believe God sees you? What are some ways that you
    can hear God's affirmations about you so that you an drown out
    the inner critic? (Day 10 questions 2 and 3)
  - What does powerlessness mean to you? (Day 11 question 1)
  - How does admitting that you're powerless to overcome your
    problems help you change? How can powerlessness be like a
    "warm blanket"? (Day 11 question 3)
  - Ask if anyone did Day 9's Going Deeper challenge and see if they
    would like to share their experience. If not, ask if anyone has
    anything to share from the Going Deeper sections.
- Encourage group members to read all of Days 13–18 and answer
  the questions at the end of each day in the blank spaces provided.
  Ask them to come next week prepared to discuss.

- Finally, close in prayer, thank them for coming, and read Zephaniah 3:17 to the group. If you know the song, close with it.

SESSION 4: CREATING CHANGE

Lesson Goal:

As a result of this session, participants will learn the principles of change. The first principle is that it's impossible to get well on your own. We need others to help us along in our process. The second principle is that we need to experience universality with others in our group. Universality brings a person out of isolation and enables him to get the encouragement, support, and accountability needed for change. By the end of this session, participants will understand how to let go of life-controlling issues that have been holding them back from the lives that they have always wanted.

Leading the Session:

- Review guidelines for a smooth small group session.
- Facilitate a brief check-in of the week and a feelings check.
- Focus on these questions for this week's lesson.
  - Why do you think it is so difficult to change on our own? (Day 13 question 1)
  - What has kept you from sharing your struggles with others? (Day 13 question 2)
  - What could be the benefits of opening up to a small group of people? (Day 13 question 3)
  - What does this current small group mean to you? (New question)
  - What dreams have you given up on after a few failed attempts? (Day 18 question 2)
  - What do you need to do to persevere? (Day 18 question 3)
- Ask them to share anything from a Going Deeper section that struck them as important or moved them in some way.
- Encourage group members to read all of Days 19–24 and answer

the questions at the end of each day in the blank spaces provided. Ask them to come next week prepared to discuss.

- Finally, close in prayer and read Hebrews 12:1–3 for encouragement.

SESSION 5: HOPE RESTORED

Lesson Goal:

As a result of this session, participants will learn that they have a "false self." They will learn why they develop this false self and how it hinders the process of change. Learning to become authentic is the goal.

Leading the Session:

- Review guidelines for a smooth small group session.
- Facilitate a brief week check-in and possible feelings check.
- Focus on these questions for this week's lesson.
  - If people knew the truth about you, would they like you? Why or why not? (Day 19 question 1)
  - How have you built up a false self to protect yourself from the pain of rejection? What would it take to begin to drop that false identity? (Day 19 question 3)
  - In what ways do you tend to put the opinions of other people before the opinion of God? How can you work to put God's opinion first? (Day 21 question 3)
  - If given the opportunity to face one of those areas [that you are afraid to face] with great courage, what would you do differently from what you are doing now? (Day 22 question 2)
  - If you could take one baby step toward change today, what would it be? (Day 23 question 3)
  - What are ways that you can look past the prison walls of your circumstance to see the hope that God has for you? (Day 24 question 3)

- Ask them to share anything from a Going Deeper section that moved them in some way. Focus on Day 20 and ask if it is hard to talk honestly with God. Give them permission to say whatever is on their hearts to God because God can handle it.
- Close in prayer, but then pair them with their accountability partners to pray openly and honestly with God.
- Encourage group members to read all of Days 25–30 and answer the questions at the end of each day in the blank spaces provided. Ask them to come next week prepared to discuss.
- Hand out one index card to each participant and tell them that they will need it for the Going Deeper section on Day 25 of next week. Ask participants to bring them back next week and be willing to share with the class.

SESSION 6: OVERCOME OBSTACLES

Lesson Goal:

As a result of this session, participants will learn how to overcome obstacles and finish their process of change with power. They will be looking at their body, mind, and spirit goals and will understand that meeting their goals is about progress, not perfection.

Leading the Session:

- Review guidelines for a smooth small group session.
- Facilitate a brief week check-in and possible feelings check.
- Focus on these questions for this week's lesson.
  - What is one positive step that you can take today to change your life for the better? (Day 26 question 3)
  - What in your life would need to be chipped away for the angel to emerge? (Day 27 question 2)
  - If you could forget your past and nothing was holding you

back, what would your life look like? (Day 27 question 3) ***Take the extra time and encourage everyone in your group to answer this question.***

- What is one goal that you have set for yourself that you have yet to achieve? What is one step that you can take today toward achieving that goal? (Day 29 question 3)
- What is really important to you? One way to know this is to think through what you would want people to say about you at your funeral. Ask them to share what they would want friends, family, co-workers, and others to say about them. (Day 30 question 2) ***Take the extra time and encourage everyone in your group to answer this question.***
- If there is time, have the group share from their Going Deeper experience. Focus on Day 28.
- Encourage group members to read all of Days 31–36 and answer the questions at the end of each day in the blank spaces provided. Ask them to come next week prepared to discuss.
- Thank everyone for coming and ask them to take out their index card from the previous week to go around and read the Bible verse that they have written on the card. Close in prayer.

SESSION 7: FINISH STRONG

Lesson Goal:

This session consists of showing participants how to further their process of change by designing personal plans of action. Making progress in their plans of action will require that they show up, do their part, and trust God with the results. This will give the members determination to stay the course, because recovery is usually two steps forward and one step back. We want to encourage them to let go of the past and make steps toward change. Stay on the course because freedom is possible. It's just around the corner.

Leading the Session:

- Review guidelines for a smooth small group session.
- Facilitate a brief week check-in and possible feelings check.
- Focus on these questions for this week's lesson.
  - What loss have you had in your life that you have been unable to grieve fully? What have you done with it until now? What steps do you need to take to begin grieving that loss in order to be able to move forward? (Day 31 questions 2 & 3)
  - What "boat" do you need to get out of in order to change? (Day 32 question 2)
  - In what situation have you experienced the joy that comes through trial and perseverance? What would getting a glimpse of your finish line mean to you? (Day 33 questions 2 & 3)
  - What are your thoughts on the process of the bee in this chapter? What could be the role of pain and struggle in your life? (Day 34 question 2)
  - Have your problems caused you to move toward God or away from Him? (Day 34 question 1)
  - Are you ready to allow God to do His work in your life? Explain why or why not. (Day 34 question 3) ***Please take the time to allow everyone to answer this question.***
- Share a Going Deeper experience that you had this past week and ask the group to share about their time, as well.
- Explain how each participant is expected to write their action plan this next week. Answer any questions that they may have pertaining to their action plan. Let the group know that by looking back through their homework, including their answers to the questions (especially the third question of each day), will help them formulate what and how they need to change and give them a jump start on this process.
- Create a sample action plan to pass out to the group in order to show how detailed the plan should be (template for action plan found in Day 35).

- Ask participants to bring copies of their action plan to pass out to other group members. This will create more accountability.
- Encourage members of the group to share their plan with one person this week before coming to class. This will help them get used to telling their story to others and not going into isolation when they find something that they want to change. Remind them that they will be sharing this action plan with the whole group.
- Thank each of them for coming and close in prayer.

SESSION 8: YOUR ACTION PLAN

This is the most important section of *Journey to Freedom*.

Leading the Session:
- Go over the group guidelines for respecting each participant as they share their plan.
- Have each participant read their action plan aloud, as well as pass a copy to each participant.
- Have them sign the place provided in their book committing them to follow this plan of action that they have created.
- Talk about the specific next steps that they can take now that the class has ended. (i.e., the next book in the *Journey to Freedom* series, twelve-steps or other recovery programs, personal training or exercise program, etc.)
- Make sure they have all the resources they need to fulfill their action plan.
- Hold hands and sing "Amazing Grace."
- Make the last meeting a celebration!
- Thank them for coming and close in prayer.

NOTES

Introduction
1. Gerald G. May, *Addiction and Grace* (San Francisco: HarperSanFrancisco, 1991), 42.
2. Luke 14:28–29
3. James O. Prochaska, John C. Norcross, and Carlo C. DiClimente, *Changing for Good* (New York: Avon Books, 1995), 15.

Day 1
1. May, 42.
2. Oswald Chambers, *My Utmost for His Highest* (Nashville: Thomas Nelson Publishers, 1992), October 10.

Day 2
1. Annie Dillard, *The Writing Life* (New York: Perennial, 1990), 105.
2. Henri Nouwen, *Seeds of Hope: A Henri Nouwen Reader* (New York: Image Books, 1997), 160.
3. Thomas Merton, *The New Man* (New York: Noonday Press, 1961), 175.
4. John Ortberg, *The Life You've Always Wanted* (Michigan: Zondervan, 2002), 130–131.
5. May, 42.

Day 3
1. Romans 8:28
2. C. S. Lewis, *The Great Divorce* (New York, NY: HarperCollins, 2001), 108.
3. John 21:5–6
4. Isaiah 43:2

Day 4
1. John Ortberg, *The Life You've Always Wanted* (Grand Rapids, Mich.: Zondervan, 1997), 42.
2. Ortberg, 43.
3. May, 73.
4. Martin E. P. Seligman, *Learned Optimism* (New York: Pocket Books, 1998), 48–49.
5. May, 1.

Day 5
1. Chip Dodd, *Voice of the Heart* (Franklin, TN: Providence House Publishers, 2001), 35.
2. Dodd, 41.
3. Matthew 21:12
4. May, 102.
5. Dodd, 62.
6. Dodd, 90.

Day 6
1. Prochaska, 81.
2. Some items in the list were adapted from Prochaska, 79.
3. Richard Leider, *The Power of Purpose: Creating Meaning in Your Life and Work* (San Francisco: Berrett-Koehler Publishers, Inc., 1997), 36–37.
4. C. S. Lewis, *The Voyage of the Dawn Treader* (New York, NY: HarperCollins, 1952), 91.
5. C. S. Lewis, 109

Day 7
1. May, 90.
2. Arthur Freeman, Ph.D., and Rose DeWolf, *Woulda, Coulda, Shoulda* (New York: William Morrow, 1989; Harper Perennial, 1990), 106.
3. Seligman, 83.
4. Freeman, 106.

5. Romans 12:2
6. Romans 12:2

Day 8
1. Thom Rutledge, *Embracing Fear and Finding the Courage to Live Your Life* (San Francisco: Harper San Francisco, 2002), 1.
2. See www.toastmasters.com.
3. Irvin D. Yalom, *Theory and Practice of Group Psychotherapy* (New York: Basic Books, 1995), 7–8.
4. Prochaska, 111.
5. Psalm 94:18
6. Jeremiah 29:11
7. Psalm 34:4

Day 9
1. See http://www.eastbayri.com/print/292213007197771.php.
2. Prochaska, 74.
3. See http://cms.psychologytoday.com/articles/index.php?term=pto-20030624-000007.
4. Prochaska, 77.
5. Psalm 139:23
6. Psalm 139:23
7. Psalm 139:124

Day 10
1. Max Lucado, with Sergio Martinez (illustrator), *You Are Special* (Wheaton, Ill.: Crossway Books, 1997).

Day 11
1. May, 24.
2. Isaiah 1:18
3. May, 19.
4. 2 Corinthians 5:17

Day 12
1. John 14:27
2. Horatio Spafford, *It Is Well with My Soul,* 1876.
3. Philippians 4:7 KJV

Day 13
1. Proverbs 28:13
2. Chuck Swindoll, *Come Before Winter,* (Portland: Multnomah Press, 1985), 36–37.

Day 14
1. 1 Corinthians 15:33
2. Henry Cloud and John Townsend, *God Will Make a Way* (Nashville: Integrity Publishers, 2002), 153.
3. George Sheehan, M.D., *Personal Best: The Foremost Philosopher of Fitness Shares Techniques and Tactics for Success and Self-Liberation* (New York: Rodale Press, 1992), 10.
4. Cloud and Townsend, 155.
5. Genesis 39:7, 12
6. Prochaska, 95.
7. 1 Corinthians 3:6

Day 15
1. Robbie Stovall story

Day 16
1. Prochaska, 79.
2. This is not a blanket endorsement for this type of surgery. There are risks involved. Please consult your doctor.
3. See Nehemiah 4.
4. Roger von Oech, *Creative Whack Pack* (Stamford, Conn.: U.S. Games Systems, Inc., Publishers, 1992), card #56.

Day 17

1. Adapted from Paul Harvey, *Paul Harvey's The Rest of the Story* (New York: Bantam, 1978), 115.
2. See 1 Kings 18:1–40; 19:1–18.
3. Hebrews 12:1

Day 18

1. Jeremiah 32:27
2. Jeremiah 29:11

Day 19

1. See http://theacc.collegesports.com/sports/m-baskbl/spec-rel/020403aah.html.
2. Prochaska, 48.
3. Of course, we don't want this to become a self-fulfilling prophecy where somewhere in the back of your mind you cause relapse to take place because you believe it's what everyone goes through. You may not. You may be successful on your first attempt.
4. Karen Horney, MD, *Our Inner Conflicts* (New York, NY: W. W. Nortion, 1992), 111.
5. Lewis Smedes, *Forgive and Forget: Healing the Hurts We Don't Deserve* (San Francisco: Harper SanFrancisco, 1984), 7.

Day 20

1. Os Guinness, *God in the Dark* (Wheaton, Ill.: Crossway Books, 1996), 62.
2. Luke 7:47
3. Hebrews 4:12
4. Matthew 23:27

Day 21

1. Jane Fonda, *My Life So Far* (New York: Random House, 2005).
2. Romans 12:2
3. Fonda, 522.
4. Dr. Harry Emerson Fosdick, *On Being a Real Person* (New York: Harper & Brothers, 1943), 61.
5. Fosdick, 63.

Day 22

1. B. B. King, *Blues All Around Me: The Autobiography of B. B. King* (New York: Avon Books, 1996), 146.
2. Dietrich Bonhoeffer, *Prisoner for God: Letters and Papers from Prison* (New York: Macmillan, 1959), 21.
3. King, 146.
4. 2 Timothy 4:6–7

Day 23

1. Jeremiah 29:11
2. Lewis B. Smedes, *How Can It Be All Right When Everything Is All Wrong?* (Colorado Springs: Shaw Publishers, 1999), 186.
3. Smedes, *How It Can Be All Right,* 187.
4. Smedes, *How It Can Be All Right,* 187.
5. W. Paul Jones, "Courage As the Heart of Faith," *Weavings—Woven Together in Love—A Journal of the Christian Spiritual Life,* 13:6.
6. 1 Corinthians 15:19
7. Job 11:18

Day 24

1. Von Oech, card #48.
2. May, 147.
3. Matthew 12:43–45
4. G. Campbell Morgan, *The Parables and Metaphors of Our Lord* (Old Tappan, NJ: Fleming H. Revell, 1943), 41.
5. 2 Corinthians 5:17

Day 25

1. John Gray, *Mars and Venus Diet and Exercise Solution* (New York, NY: St. Martins Press, 2002), 43.

Day 26
1. Genesis 32:28
2. Prochaska, 75.
3. Used by permission from the *YMCA Activating America* campaign.
4. Matthew 11:28
5. Matthew 19:26

Day 27
1. Robbie Stovall Story
2. Philippians 3:13–14
3. 2 Corinthians 5:17
4. Galatians 5:22
5. Proverbs 29:18 KJV

Day 28
1. Nehemiah 4:2–3
2. "So we built the wall, and the entire wall was joined together up to half its height, for the people had a mind to work" (Neh. 4:6 NKJV).
3. Nehemiah 4:10
4. Rick Warren, *Answers to Life's Difficult Questions* (Wheaton, Ill.: Victor Books, 1985), 67.
5. May, 42.

Day 29
1. Dr. Patrick Carnes, *A Gentle Path through the Twelve Steps* (Center City, Minn.: Hazeldon, 1993), 1
2. Charles Reynolds Brown, *Finding Ourselves* (New York: Harper & Brothers, 1935), 9.
3. Hebrews 12:1
4. Brown, 11.

Day 30
1. Luke 9:23–24 NIV

Day 31
1. Cloud and Townsend, 52.
2. Matthew 19:26 KJV
3. Romans 8:28

Day 32
1. Matthew 14:27
2. Matthew 14:28–29
3. John Maxwell, *Failing Forward* (Nashville: Thomas Nelson, 2000), 127.
4. Michael P. Green, *Illustrations for Biblical Preaching* (Grand Rapids, Mich.: Baker Books, 1991), 52.

Day 33
1. Green, 264.
2. James 1:2–3 NKJV
3. Leider, 26.
4. James 1:4 NKJV
5. James 5:7–8
6. Kenny Moore, "A Long Run Gets Longer," *Sports Illustrated*, July 22, 1992, 94.
7. Galatians 6:9 NKJV

Day 34
1. Matthew 11:28
2. 1 John 4:18
3. May, 140.

CONTINUING YOUR JOURNEY TO FREEDOM

As you continue in pursuit of the person God created
you to be, you may find these books helpful, as well:

The Journey to a Life of Significance:
Freedom from a Low Self-Esteem

This guide will lead you from living with crippling low self-esteem to the freedom of hope and confidence. This probing
guide is about learning to break free from physical and emo-tional issues that can lead to depression and a myriad of other
addictions.

The Journey to Healthy Living:
Freedom from Body Image and Food Issues

This guide will help you release the intense burden of being
controlled by food and physical appearance. It helps you learn
how to deal with life-controlling food issues, no matter what
they are—weight loss, eating disorders, food addictions, or
body image issues.

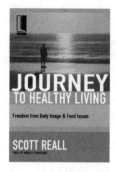

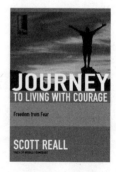

The Journey to a New Beginning After Loss:
Freedom from the Pain of Disappointment

There is a way through loss. Be it loss of a loved one, loss of a
dream, loss of a relationship, or the many other losses we can
experience, this guide can be the beginning of help, hope, and
healing. You will learn to deal with loss in healthy ways and
learn how to experience life again.

Journey to Living with Courage:
Freedom from Fear

It's one of the most important journeys we can take in life: the
journey away from fear. Life is too short and too amazing for
any of us to live in the grip of chronic fear. Learn how to move
from a fear-based life to a faith-based life—a life grounded in
the courage and freedom only God offers.

*Please visit **www.journeytofreedom.org** for more information
on the Journey to Freedom series.*